The Intrigue of
Small Thoughts

Pathway to a Deeper Life

Margi Deeks

I dedicate this book to the pride and joy of my life, my eleven grandchildren: Sidney, Macien, Emmi, Sadie, Ella, Cameron, Molly, Kayleigh, Max, Chase, and Elijah.

Show me the right path, O Lord;
point out the road for me to follow.
Lead me by your truth, and teach me.

(Psalm 25:4–5 NLT)

May you always choose to follow Jesus. I love you so much. My prayers go with you.

—Gigi

Acknowledgments

My first gratitude belongs to Jesus. His Word, the Bible, has shaped my life and my writing. With Him by my side, my words take flight.

My husband, Chuck, stands tall and tops my thank-you list. His greatest gift is helping others. He's my best friend and teammate, and he has capably taken over kitchen duty to free me to write. This book is in your hands because of his encouragement and enthusiasm for getting it into print.

To our three children, Brian, Danae (Geoffrey), and Bret (Kristin). You make my heart sing! There is no greater joy than knowing you all walk with Jesus. The best role in my world is being a mom. Now inching its way to a tie is being gigi to our eleven grandchildren. My cup overflows. Thank you for being my robust cheerleaders!

To Dad and Mom, who are now enjoying heaven. Thank you for introducing me to Jesus. Your love for God's Word and for people rubbed off on me. You set the example, and I believe you were welcomed into heaven with these words: "Well done, my faithful servants." I aspire to be like you.

I want to thank the artist who designed my cover. Jess Van Lehn beautifully captured what I imagined. I highly recommend her work. Her contact information is on the copyright page. The cover contains significant details: the willow tree is a childhood memory, the bluebird is my favorite bird (and it's my husband's too), and a goldendoodle lives at each of our grandchildren's homes. The scene portrays a storied life.

Lastly, I wish I could list the names of all who encouraged my writing over the years. You know who you are—a deep, heartfelt thanks for each comment you shared with me. Your comments added up, and here we are! A book that you helped write.

I'm humbled and grateful and a wee bit amazed.

—Margi

Introduction

When I pick up a book to read, the pages I am most interested in are at the beginning. Who is this author?

Before I get to the beginning, allow me to start at the end. When my life comes to a close, my desire is to be remembered as one who shone the love of Jesus. And that is why I wrote this book. It is not a Bible study book, nor is it a devotional book. It is a peek into my heart, a conversation that if you were sitting nook-side with me, these words would tumble out. It is my small attempt to inspire a deeper life, beginning with my own.

So who am I?

I live at Wander Inn Cottage in Ohio with my husband of thirty-nine years. Our empty nest is often filled with our three adult children, their spouses, and our eleven grandchildren. God has given me abundantly more than I ever prayed for.

Although I'm an introvert, I love connecting with people. One compliment I received for my writing perfectly reflects my heart's desire:

"When I read your words, I feel like we are journeying along life's path together." That is a good summary of why I write. We don't travel alone.

God has given me wonderful opportunities, including leading Bible studies, writing, church ministry, and using our home for hospitality. My calling includes the anything-but-ordinary high privilege of being a wife, mom, and gigi. As I lean into all that God has for me, I find that the ordinary is truly extraordinary.

Those who know me well know it is not an exaggeration that I have a poor sense of direction. There is a medical term for it: developmental topographical disorientation (DTD). This neurological condition causes people to be unable to hold maps or directions in their minds.

I share that only to share this: I may feel hopelessly lost when out on the highways, but when it comes to what matters in life, I assuredly know the map. I refer to it often in my writing. It is the Bible. And the author is Jesus. You don't have to be acquainted with either to read this book. I pray that you will gain a nugget of truth for your life or, at the least, a smile. At the end of the book, if interested, there is an explanation of how you can learn more about what it means to follow Jesus.

As I opened my laptop to begin day one of this book-writing task, I reminded myself that each keystroke was part of my story and part of yours. We may not share a keyboard, but we can share a walk.

I would love to hear from you, my reader, about your journey and your small thoughts. I promise to answer every response. Thank you for your gift of presence with me. My contact information is on the back cover of the book.

Grab your water bottle. Let's meet for the next seventy-five days. Happy hiking!

A Tale of Two Homes

All the rooms in our bed-and-breakfast were filled this past weekend. Since this was our first full booking, I scribbled a few reflections into my notebook:

- Buy more towels. Eighteen white towels are not enough.
- The Crock-Pot is my new best friend. I need to expand my menu.
- There are a lot of nice people in the world. We traveled to the Philippines without leaving our family room.
- Coffee, anyone? Coffee? Coffee?

After our nest was emptied at our previous home, my husband and I renovated the second story into a four-bedroom spa-like B&B, primarily for missionaries. In discussing our idea, a friend asked, "Since this is a no-charge venture, isn't it going to get expensive?" Before I could respond, I heard Dad's words: "God keeps the books."

I wonder if our friends secretly thought it was a (1) crazy idea, (2) dud idea, or (3) never-get-off-the-ground idea. A peek into my heart reveals (1), (2), and (3). But if God could take my crazy idea, keep it from dudding out, and bring it to reality—imagine what He can do for you. Or what He is already doing for you!

I'm not sure if any of you have ever dreamed of being an innkeeper. I believe God wants to astonish us with something incredible and fulfilling in our lives. Dream a little. Pray even bigger. And then pay attention to that small stirring of hope and vision deep down inside. Because we are created in God's image, our lives are meant to brim and overflow with creativity in thousands of ways.

PS: After thirty-six years in our home with the added B&B, we downsized to a small ranch. Gone are the five bedrooms with four baths. In its place . . . well, keep reading, and you'll see what the Lord has done for us.

Our address changed, but not my innkeeping title. We now reside at Wander Inn Cottage.

Connecting the Dots

Dot A: They looked more like models on the cover of a family magazine than missionaries traveling to South Africa. Richard and Megan, with their four young sons, entered our lives one ordinary weekend. It took less than five minutes to catch their passion and love for the people of Lesotho. Using aviation, they planned to bring hope to this poverty-ridden mountainous country with medical help and food. We were happy to provide housing for this family for a short time.

Dot B: My background is mission-directed. My life has revolved around missions, from my mission-minded parents to my pursuit of a mission degree and my added years of working in a mission agency. My plan A had been to be a missionary on foreign soil. God had a better plan.

Dot C: There are rare and special moments of clarity in life. The curtain is pulled back, and you can view the panoramic view of your life as God must see it.

As is our ritual, with luggage in hand, we walked the missionary family out to their van. We gave warm hugs and a bag of chocolate chip cookies. As I tearfully watched Richard and Megan drive away, that moment of clarity arrived. I may not have ended up on foreign soil, but I have the honor and privilege of serving those who do.

Serving the servants—the dots are connected. A little part of my heart would be flying in a Cessna 206 Turbo over the mountainous regions of South Africa. Meanwhile, I have my own mountain of white sheets and towels to climb.

$1.90 Bargain

Lunchtime is often a green salad and a piece of fruit or soup. On this particular summer day in 2010, I found my way to the Golden Arches.

"One hamburger and one small fry," I ordered.

"That will be $1.90," muffled the invisible order-taker.

What did I get for $1.90? A warmed-up flattened-out hamburger. And wimpy fries.

Opening the bag, suddenly I was eight again, where opening up the Golden Arches bag was a family highlight of our month. It was an after-church treat. The rules came flooding back: pick two. You can't have a pop, fries, and a hamburger. Pick two: Dad's rule.

What did I get for $1.90?

Wrapped inside that not-so-tasty-or-nutritious meal was a link to a treasured memory. Remembering Dad's voice. And a link to other "rules"—important principles to guide us when we might start losing our way. A voice who knew the best advice wasn't his; it was advice found in the living words, the Bible. The Rule Book turned Grace Book.

Grace. Dad's words. My Bible.

I got my money's worth that day. And I'd like to think that if Dad were there, he, too, would say about the long-ago Golden Arch lunches, "So did I, Monkey, so did I."

PS: When I was a young girl, Dad said I could climb trees faster than my brothers. He nicknamed me Monkey Jo. Over the years, it got shortened to Monk, a nickname still used by my husband. Should you like to email me, I will answer you at monkjo@live.com.

Eight Legs

Arachnids. Congregating in our bedroom! Sisters, brothers, cousins, aunts, and uncles were having a spider reunion at my house. My apologies, Charlotte of the Web, for hurting your sensibilities, but I do not like your friends, especially the ones the size of a quarter with fur.

I was mystified, losing track after flushing down number thirteen. It was time to seek hubby's help to solve the eight-legged mystery.

Two days and several more spiders later, I carefully tiptoed to my bathroom. Peeking out from behind the toilet was an eight-legged, wait for it, blue plastic spider planted by hubs, who totally missed the urgency of the mission.

Later that evening, hubby turned on the Yankee's baseball game. I resigned to living on tiptoes, opened my Kindle, and settled in for a read.

I opened one of the books I was reading by Warren Wiersbe, *10 People Every Christian Should Know.*

Enter Jonathan Edwards, 1703–1758, a quiet scholar who preached one of the most famous sermons ever preached in America. He had one

Intrigue of Small Thoughts

purpose: to shake people out of their religious complacency. At age nineteen, he began a list of resolutions to read weekly as a compass to guide him. I continued gleaning information about this preacher, and I kid you not, one of his passionate interests was WATCHING SPIDERS!

I saw God smiling.

Dear Jonathan, I don't share your passion for spiders. Still, I would do well to share your passion for Resolution #28: "Resolved, to study the Scriptures so steadily, constantly, and frequently, as that I may find, and plainly perceive, myself to grow in the knowledge of the same."[1]

You were a man who loved God and longed more than anything to glorify Him. Mr. Edwards, I am pleased to meet you.

As to our spiders, we have included pest control in our inn's yearly budget. So done with eight legs.

Signed, Innkeeper

I Don't Want to Forget

I am home, standing before the mirror, washing off traces of what is left of my makeup. I stop for a minute and look into my eyes—eyes tonight that have seen too much of life's ugly side. Eyes that will soon close in needed prayer and rest.

My husband and I spent the past five hours in the presence of three transitional homeless families. We read books and played games with precious, lively children. I was privileged to bottle-feed a sweet baby boy. We shared our homemade supper with them. And while crunching on tacos, we heard their stories.

Three moms who live in a world vastly unlike mine, a world that I can't fix. The best we could do was what we did: mostly listen.

I offered a few affirmations of how far they had come this past year and how hard they had worked in their parenting class or said, "Good job, you made it twenty months drug-free."

Before we slipped out the door, I hugged them, and in a quiet spirit of love, I shared with them about Someone who loves and cares about them. Briefly, I shared that though my struggles look different than theirs, I still need hope, and I find it in Jesus.

"Can I sit next to you?"

This question was from a little girl with dark eyes and twenty-five colorful barrettes bouncing around her head. She will never know how her one small question stirred my heart, twirled around in my mind, and settled into my soul.

Yes. There is room for you, little girl. You can happily sit next to me.

Because Jesus gave me a seat at the table, I am compelled to invite others to join. Hope is served to broken people, people like me, and three moms on the other side of the world.

An Artist's Language

I saw a delicate flower grown up 2 feet high;
Between the horse's path & the wheel track.
Which Dakin's & Maynards wagons
had passed over many a time
An inch more to right or left had sealed its fate,
Or an inch higher. And yet it lived and flourish[e]d
As much as if it had a thousand acres
Of untrodden space around it—and never
Knew the danger it incurred.

—Henry David Thoreau

If I were an artist, I would paint this quote and title it *Blooming on a Thousand Acres.*

It makes you wonder how pressed in Henry was by the cares and dangers of his 1800s world.

I am studying the life of Moses. For those unfamiliar with this Old Testament giant, he was both palace and desert trained when God called him to rescue the Israelites from slavery. It would require bold courage in the face of significant opposition.

With all his training, Moses should have moved forward with great confidence. Yet he felt woefully inadequate. (I'm with ya, Moses.) But time after time, God showed up, just as He promised.

I found a detail on Moses' leadership in Hebrews 11. Moses persevered because he saw Him who is invisible. In his line of vision, it was not the mighty, ungodly Pharoah but God who shepherded him.

Interestingly, Henry David Thoreau was best known for advocating his belief in transcendentalism and self-reliance. Moses was the opposite— he was best known as a man of faith, not in himself but in God.

Our Wander Inn Cottage sits on a one-third-acre lot. But the reality? I live on 1,000 acres, just like the flower in my painting. Yes, we are pressed in by the cares of this world. But I'm finding acres and acres of space—freedom, peace, comfort, purpose, courage, and wisdom— walking with Jesus. Come step into my painting and bloom with me.

The Chosen

Nervously, we walked into the courthouse, prepared to place a bid on a house at a sheriff's auction. It was our first auction, and it was a daring move to bid on a house without first being allowed access to the inside.

The room filled up. Our turn finally arrived. The bidding began, and within minutes, we won the bid. We were hopeful owners of our second home in our married life. The next step was to wait for the deed to clear all the red tape, which took months. While nervously waiting for the deed to become ours, I named the house Wander Inn Cottage.

In our quest to downsize from our home of thirty-six years, after patience-testing months, we finally received the call to collect the deed. A walk-through confirmed what we guessed: a total house rehab would be necessary. We were excited, as we sensed God's peace leading us to this exact location.

Wander Inn Cottage. The name resonates even more today as we stroll through the village, meet our neighbors, and invite them for coffee and dessert. It is thrilling to open our doors to young couples, elderly folks, and all the in-betweens. For house number two, finding a sense of community was important to us. We asked the Lord to place us where we could make new friends and share His love and hope.

At Wander Inn, I like to say we are living big in the small. Although our ranch home is much smaller than our previous five-bedroom, four-bath home, it is uniquely designed for sharing hospitality. We have a better playroom setup. It is more than sufficient for our needs, and we love it. Our nook window looks out to a beautiful line of woods. We can walk right down the middle of the street. I sense God winks at His choice for us.

For exterior colors, I chose white siding with bright red shutters. We expanded our front porch to welcome passersby and dog walkers. And by our front door, in red scripted metal, hangs this sign: Wander Inn Cottage. This is your invitation to wander in! Look for the red chimney.

A Habit of Order

If a task can be completed in one minute, do it. I am working on this habit. It only takes a minute to knock down a couple of cobwebs, sort a kitchen towel drawer, or shine a sink. It amazes me how much one can accomplish in such a short time.

My spice drawer organizing didn't make the minute timer, but still, it took no more than twenty minutes. The finished project is a beauty to behold. The little glass jars are lined up and perfectly labeled alphabetically. Each time I open this drawer, it gives me delight.

Why do I care so much about order? Perhaps because so much of life is beyond my control, but this little spice space I can control. And I have high hopes that if my spices are well ordered, so is my life. A tall order? Yup.

I chose this guiding life verse many years ago in Bible college: "He has shown you [Margi] what is good; And what does the Lord require of you but to do justly, To love mercy, And to walk humbly with your God?" (Micah 6:8 NKJV).

There is nary a mention of well-organized spices.

Intrigue of Small Thoughts

However, the opposite of organization is a lot of clutter. Clutter occurs in our lives, beyond counters, closets, and cabinets. Do you feel it too?

I've been working on that well-ordered list from Micah, a prophet of God. And I have a long way to go. At the end of his book, Micah pointed God's people toward an everlasting hope in an everlasting God. Reminder: we do not walk alone. I'm creating habits of order at the inn.

I do see Jesus smile as He looks over my spice space.

Dad Would Have Loved It

Every Thanksgiving, I pause to remember and give thanks for my dad, a dad who gave his daughter everything she needed to live life without him. He introduced me to Jesus. He instilled in me a love for God's Word. He exemplified what it means to walk steadily with Jesus and share His love with others.

It's hard to believe it has been twenty-two years since Dad has been missing from our table. In the years of his absence, he missed meeting thirteen people: our children's spouses and our grandchildren. And that saddens me.

Dad would have surely loved them.

My husband often talks about how my dad was his mentor. As Chuck leads our Thanksgiving gathering in prayer, I can't help but think about Dad's influence. Chuck carries on Dad's tradition and legacy.

Dad would have loved it.

As part of our Thanksgiving celebration, our grandchildren recreate a flannelgraph story of "Only One." In the Bible account in Luke 17, Jesus healed ten men of leprosy. Nine men went on their merry way, distracted by their gift. Only one returned to pour out his heart and give Jesus thanks. We rehearsed the lesson.

Dad would have loved it.

Bundle up! The last of our Thanksgiving traditions is a walk. This year, it is a walk around the village—a Thanksgiving Day parade of eighteen.

> *Let us come before His presence with thanksgiving;*
> *Let us shout joyfully to Him with psalms.*
>
> (Psalm 95:2 NKJV)

At the inn, we've got the joyful noise down.

Dad would have loved it.

A Walk to Remember

There were days along the shores of Kitty Hawk, NC, when the view was clear and seemingly endless. We enjoyed a daily stroll along with a morning hike to Duck Donuts while vacationing for a week with family and friends.

One afternoon, the fog rolled in. The abrupt change in just a day was amazing. The dense fog on the ocean was unlike anything I had ever seen before. I could not see ten feet ahead of myself. The visibility was unbelievably low.

I told my husband, "It reminds me of faith. You can only see enough to take one step forward." The unknown, the uncertainty, lay off in the distance. It looked scary and daunting.

I looked down on our walk and picked up a few reminders—small pebbles beaten smooth by the waves. I needed to be reminded about my own faith walk and the certainty that, in the thick fog, I could trust Jesus.

Predecide. Embrace the changes. There are enough circumstances in my life to keep me whispering prayers.

Faith. Just one step. I choose to rest in the murky waters. Jesus holds me in the midst of the hard.

These things I remember
as I pour out my soul.

(Psalm 42:4 NIV)

Faith sustains in the most trying places. I walk amongst seashells accompanied by peace. And watch the fog lift.

A Special Valentine

Romance is in the air. The calendar and shopping aisles declare pink and red, hearts and lace.

As I look back over the thirty-eight years of marking Valentine's Days, I see a blur of nice dinners and flowers. But there is one Valentine's Day that rises above all the rest.

It was 1992. We had three children, ages seven, five, and three. Through a winding, complicated story, God amazed us with baby number four on the way. We had gotten our miracle! The pregnancy was familiar, like all the rest, in and out of the hospital, getting hooked up to IVs to treat extreme morning sickness.

Until February 14, 1992. The heartbeat was lost. There would be no miracle baby to hold. A D&C procedure, a hospital bracelet, and broken hearts were the only proof that our baby existed.

In deep grief, God gave me a verse I had never connected with. I struggled to memorize it, so I printed it out on a 3x5 card and, for many nights, slept with it under my pillow.

Intrigue of Small Thoughts

"For I know the plans I have for you," says the Lord.
"They are plans for good and not for disaster,
to give you a future and a hope."

(Jeremiah 29:11 NLT)

God gave my husband and me a beautiful gift on that long-ago Valentine's Day, a gift that outshines all the others. Our Valentine's baby taught us about trusting God when we didn't understand, when life was not served up according to our dreams. The greatest lesson was found in these words: I have a plan for you, and it's good.

My vision of having six children had ended. God had placed a period. But in its place, He gave us peace. An incredible peace that would carry us into all the years to follow, seasons of more plans and dreams that didn't always measure up.

We have learned to trust His plan. It has taken a lot of practice. Somedays, we still reach for that 3x5 card.

February 14, 1992. Grief turned into hope, and hope turned into deep faith. Deep faith keeps two sweethearts connected and very much in love.

This Valentine's Day, we celebrate with steak and apple pie. Sweet are the memories, and sweeter still, someday, we will hold baby number four.

I have a plan for you.

Oaks, Elephants, and Single Digits

Little strokes fell great oaks.

—Benjamin Franklin

Why, hello, Benjamin Franklin.

I designed my one-a-days because (1) my house was getting messy behind closed cabinets, closets, and doors and (2) hiring a maid was not in the budget. A purge was needed as well as an old-fashioned cleaning.

I walked around the inn, listing every closet, drawer, cabinet, floor, surface, vanity, and appliance, creating a list of seventy-seven specific indoor home areas.

We've all heard how you eat the elephant one bite at a time. I did not need to finish off the elephant in any particular order. My goal was to check off one project each day. In my dedicated project, the only cleaning tool I purchased was a new fan duster; it's still a neck-ache, but it beats me falling off a stool.

As I daily checked off my list, the satisfaction meter rose. Every checkmark was a big win. I'm not saying this one-a-day project would be categorized as hard by world standards, but as I was about to cross the victory line, I could hear it: scores of applause and cheers for my seventy-seven days!

Oaks felled and an elephant eaten—a faithful job.

Remaining steadfast—it hearkens back to an old-fashioned idea. I'm grateful for a faithful, steadfast husband but even more for the faithfulness of my best friend, Jesus. One day, I aim to hear His words, "Well done, Innkeeper."

Closing in on the finish line left me twelve months to work on my budget to hire housekeeping. Of course, you know I'm kidding about the maid.

If only.

Gaining

It is said that micromanagement is the destroyer of momentum.

Micromanage is a negative term in the business world. It means to control every small part.

It's a problem in the workplace, and I'm wondering if the same could be said of micromanaging our personal lives. The problem asserts itself as we manage our to-do lists.

Our phones and computers are associated with a bazillion tasks: managing photos, files, contacts, contracts, calendars, emails, notes, finances, office work, paperwork, health, nutrition, diet, supplements, and smartwatches.

You get the picture. Most of those areas are necessary, but I find myself getting carried away with the minutiae. I could spend hours organizing the trivial.

Off in the distance, I hear a faint voice, an elderly voice with a ring of conviction. (I won't change her name because she would be honored to know I passed along her sage wisdom given to me, a new mom.)

Intrigue of Small Thoughts

Mrs. Olsen, a dear family friend, said, "Spend your life, Margi, on what is important. I wasted too much time washing walls and turning mattresses."

I never forgot that conversation, or her precious life and well-worn Bible. I can spend truckloads of time compulsively wasting time. I can care too much for the small matters that matter little in the long run.

A life that counts. I think it's what we all want.

I'm picking up momentum. My steps are taking me in the right direction, away from turning mattresses.

A Beam of Light

I found a sweet little lamp that needed a new home. I happened to have a quiet corner tucked alongside our blue-and-green guest bedroom, and the small light brightens up that little corner.

My memory slips back a few years. A call came from our church: would we be willing to house a woman in our home for a few days? We were a bit apprehensive but said yes. The woman was temporarily homeless. She needed a friend. After a few hours in her company, I suspected she needed to see that not all men were evil.

For three days, my light shone in her corner of the world. Her words became my most precious entry in our guest book: "Thank you for three days of peace."

Peace. Could there be any better gift to share? In our conversations, I found a tough and mean world that I lived sheltered from. This woman had experienced things I couldn't begin to imagine. I listened to trouble after very real trouble, just letting her talk. She finished her frightening story.

Feeling very much out of my depth to give her any counsel, I asked her if I could pray with her. I did. Then I asked if I could share a story with a happy ending. It was a joy to tell her about Jesus and His love for her.

I'm not sure what happened to this woman in all these years since, but I hope I meet her in heaven one day.

I was honored to have her company. She said I was a gift to her. I smiled. She was God's gift to me.

As I waved goodbye to her, this little Sunday school tune was humming in my heart: "This little light of mine, I'm gonna let it shine."

Brighten your corner, sweet lamp.

Master Plan

In just a blink of an eye, Christmas is here. You are cordially invited to pull up a chair, snuggle up in a cozy throw, sip hot chocolate with me, and munch on carrot sticks. Tell me, how do you keep "the most wonderful time of the year" wonderful?

I have devised a plan for December, and it looks like this:

- Limit store browsing.
- Do Advent Bible study daily.
- Walk more.
- Eat less.
- Clear up, clean up, show up, and share up.

Oh, and don't give up. The winter weight has begun to creep in, er, more like settle in.

I'm reminded, for the hundredth time, that most of us don't need a breakthrough. What we need is follow-through.

On a particularly bleak day, I looked out the window and spied a brave little pink rosebud peeking out from under the last blanket of snow.

Sometimes inspiration and beauty are found in the most unexpected places. Behind the pain, or the drain, or the complain, joy battles its way through.

Joy arrived some 2,000 years ago in a most unexpected place: a lowly manger. His name is Jesus, Immanuel, God with us, and so He is with us on the best and worst of days.

I have added this to my December checklist: savor the wonder of Jesus. Christmas is God's extravagant gift given to us in the person of His Son, Jesus. That gift changes everything. Joy bubbles up.

Tidings of great joy are parked in the very midst of your life's circumstances. It's a grand plan wrapped with a green-and-red bow.

The Tale of a Brown Shoe

Once upon a time, I had a great pair of brown shoes. These shoes had taken me to faraway places and to work. They looked great and felt great. They were temporarily tucked away in the seasonal closet to make room for sandal-wearing days.

The season passed. And by and by, I donned my brown slacks and brown shoes. Surprise! Gone was the lovely white stitching on the shoe, and in its place was a rip that grew one-half inch bigger upon each wearing. Alas, the time finally arrived to do some brown shoe shopping.

On Friday, my shopping day, an unexpected opportunity knocked at my office door. I had the privilege of being a small help to a dear missionary couple. It was specific help that was needed that day of that week. It was the kind of help that necessitated opening my purse and placing my shoe money into their hands. It was a more joyous occasion than going brown shoe shopping.

The very next day, my husband announced that he'd had several bags of hand-me-down clothing given to us, and one was for me. (This was quite an out-of-the-ordinary announcement.) I opened the bag. Blue shoes, black shoes, taupe shoes—all that I liked, but not one fit. I continued

Intrigue of Small Thoughts

digging and found in the middle of that bag a perfectly new-looking pair of brown shoes—shoes in the style I would have chosen myself.

I felt a little Cinderella-ish as I slid my foot into the brown shoe. I should not have been surprised at the perfect fit. Upon further investigation, not only was it my perfect size—it was name brand, a more expensive shoe than I was planning to buy.

Not only did Cinderella gain one pair of brown shoes, behold! There, buried in the bag, was one more perfect fit: a pair of lovely dress-up brown shoes with a small stylish bow.

> *Now all glory to God, who is able, through his mighty power at work within us, to accomplish infinitely more than we might ask or think.*
>
> (Ephesians 3:20 NLT)

My double blessing. Is God not amazing? He cares about shoe colors. I have four brown shoes to prove it!

True story.

Up in the Air

Well, not literally. I've not flown this day to a tropical climate with sandy beaches (only in my wishes). This is a more grounded kind of up-in-the-air, aptly named indecision.

For years, I debated purchasing a food processor. I had never owned or operated one, but I caught the bug to grate cabbage for coleslaw, minus the grater box, which is among my least favorite kitchen tools. (A kind neighbor had given me a used processor. In trying to figure out how it worked without a manual, hubs ended the dream.)

So my conundrum. Years ago, I read an article about ownership and overstuffing a house. One point stayed with me. Every purchase you make costs you long after the bill is paid. Ouch!

The costs can run high in real estate: where is this item going to be stored, how much room will it take, and how much maintenance will it require? For example, consider a new fifty-foot boat. Do you own the boat, or does the boat own you? Each of us weighs the cost.

Off the waterfront and back to my kitchen. As for space on my countertops, my KitchenAid mixer, Cuisinart air fryer, and Keurig coffee maker are the beginning and end of my countertop appliances. (Only in my dreams are my counters clear of appliances.)

Running through my mind were images of freshly baked blueberry zucchini bread followed by chocolate zucchini bread. I'm quite sure those recipes, not the cabbage coleslaw, prompted the purchase. Months later, having fun baking my loaves, I came to this conclusion—having hubs shred the zucchini was far easier and required less cleanup.

A year has passed since the food processor was used, meaning it has been moved out of the kitchen into storage for One Day. That One Day, when I decide to bake mountains and mountains of zucchini bread, I will be ready!

A Steep Climb

When I was a child, I spent a lot of time in the hills of Pennsylvania. Our family now owns a cabin on those hills surrounded by twenty-five acres. It was a beautiful summer day when I stopped to take a picture of the steep and long hill we used to climb as children.

Climbing demands all we have physically, mentally, emotionally, and spiritually.

Perhaps you, like me, can identify with some of the following: loneliness, broken dreams, financial distress, a child running from God, cancer, a spiritual desert, job uncertainty, addiction, a failed relationship, chronic pain, loss of loved ones . . .

Whew! I'm out of breath just writing this list. Yet I know someone in the "climb of their life" in each of those categories mentioned above. I find my name by too many. And this list could go on and on.

But every climb needs a rest stop.

When our family experienced a heartbreaking, turbulent time a few years ago, I was asked why we didn't do something, such as put in more effort.

While not offended by their question, here is my response taken from my journal.

> *Rest is our action verb. Prayer is our weapon. Resting is trusting in a God who is bigger than the challenge before us. Resting is releasing our heartache into God's care. It may appear that we are doing nothing, but as we rest and trust and pray, we wage war against the enemy.*

Sometimes climbing involves simply standing still.

Hear the words from Jeremiah, one of the great prophets of the Old Testament who was well acquainted with steep climbs:

> *I will refresh the weary and satisfy the faint.*
>
> (Jeremiah 31:25 NIV)

I remember lying in the grass as a child, watching the clouds. No matter where the climbs in life take us, look up. If your hill is too steep and you need a walking partner, Jesus offers Himself.

And then there is your fellow trekker who shares the hike with you. Together, we can make it to the top!

Simplified

In our renovated downsized new home, I decided it was time to simplify the Christmas decorations. I was reminded of the three wise men (technically, we do not know if that is an accurate number), but I decided, as keeper of the inn, that my Christmas decor had to fit into three tubs.

I chose only a few places to decorate our new home. My goal: capture the imaginations of all who enter, think many little grands. On our fireplace mantel, a winter zebra dressed in a wool coat presides over a little white house with forty-three windows and a bright red roof. The kitchen island magically transports you to a snowy winter vignette as a sweet chubby bird dressed in plaid pulls a red wagon filled with ice diamonds.

It wasn't hard to figure out where to place our newly purchased tree. Our previous tree was weary and chose to retire before our move. We shopped around until we found the perfect tree. Rather, the tree with hundreds of tiny twinkly lights found us. The sweet meetup moment happened in Walmart, aisle T-138.

Intrigue of Small Thoughts

We put Tree up, and the hundreds of tiny lights twinkled. It was love at first sight. Tree felt at home in the inn. I pulled out several bins and began decorating—red and white ornaments. I stood afar. The hundreds of tiny lights dimmed. I switched Tree to another color theme. I stood afar. The hundreds of tiny lights dimmed. A third try was made. "Oi," said the innkeeper. The tiny lights had dimmed once again. Hmm . . .

Tree got un-decorated, and the hundreds of tiny lights once again twinkled. "Aah," said the innkeeper, with her own twinkle in her eye. The tiny twinkle lights *are* the decoration.

It is one of the glories of this innkeeper to create a home that offers a warm welcome, a place that says, "Come, take a break from the storms of life." Candlelight, books to browse, laughter in the cozy, and shared notes of blessings.

And Tree, standing tall and erect, is doing its main job—shining bright—reminding the innkeeper of her main job—to shine bright. How easily her light can be dimmed by too much, just like Tree.

Distractions, fear, loss of focus, forgetting, and willful neglect. And my light dims. What's an innkeeper to do? As it happens, long and far away ago, these words were written just for the innkeeper's heart. Jesus said, "I am the light of the world" (John 8:12 NIV).

Forgive my casual speech, but hangin' with Jesus keeps my light bright. The innkeeper's habit is to stay close to the Light by reading God's Love Letter, the Bible, every morning. What we invest in becomes most precious to us.

It is a simple prayer often whispered at the inn. "May I reflect the beauty of Jesus."

All my simplified decor will fit into my three new red bins. What won't fit because it can't be contained: my own little light.

A Journal Entry

What am I holding on to? What am I letting go of? Two questions out of my *Define My Day* journal.

You've heard it said that action produces traction. Clearly stated. Now to practice. That's the hard part.

I remember struggling in the two-year season when I shared the care for my dear mom, who had terminal cancer. While being a caretaker was the role I could and wanted to carry, I missed my own rhythms. I missed being in my new home for lengthy periods each day. I missed the unhurried pace of my former life before Mom's cancer.

Some days, with a migraine for company, I looked for an exit off the merry-go-round. And I found no exit. Do you ever feel that way? You just gotta get through it, whatever your it is.

No matter how long or tiring the days were, the wrist bracelet I bought during my mom's care always reminded both Mom and me to keep going and not give up. "Never quit," said bracelet. (Looking back at the years of caring for my mom, I'm so glad for the honor. Mom is enjoying heaven now, and in my heart, I know I did my best. I only wish she were here now to hold this book in her hands.)

I'm both holding on and letting go.

Out of the ancient words in Nehemiah 8:10 comes another succinctly stated counsel: "The joy of the Lord is your strength" (KJV).

Joy in God's goodness builds traction. My morning aim is to smile more before God.

Since riding the merry-go-round in that two-year season, I have a new appreciation for some pretty great friends—God's gifts, really. I hope you have friends like that.

Better still is this prayer. Lord, help me be a friend who gives the gift of understanding. It is priceless.

White and Puffy

It sounds a bit like a description of yours truly. I struggle with extra pounds. It is a lifelong challenge. (If you wrestle with a hard-to-fix challenge, know you are in good company.) But let's move on to a cheerier topic.

Think marshmallows, not Margi.

When my kids were young, I watched Martha Stewart, America's leading cook at the time, make marshmallows. She made it look easy and fun. She also said you hadn't lived if you had not tasted homemade marshmallows versus the store-bought ones.

Many years later, to remedy my many years un-lived, I bring you marshmallows from the inn.

The ingredients were inexpensive, and the process checked the fun factor box. The gelatin changed as the syrup mixture was added, transforming into billowy white mounds. And they grew. And grew some more. The KitchenAid ran for twelve minutes, whipping the white. I felt transported back to my high school science lab.

Finishing the process of these fluffy whites was a bit tricky. The recipe warned that time was of the essence. Do not even think about scraping the bowl. (FYI, I found there is no scraping in marshmallow fluff.)

Now measure out patience. Must wait 'til morning for the final step.

It's 7 am. Excitement mounts; after all, it's been sixty-one years that Innkeeper has waited for this moment. Will it or won't it resemble anything like her Martha memory?

Drumroll . . . YES! Innkeeper takes a bow. And according to my grands' pleas for "just one more," I'm sure they heartily agree with Martha. You haven't lived until you've had a white and puffy.

May your day be filled with sweetness, not necessarily the kind that adds another pound.

Pull up a Chair

I read of a grandma who was dearly loved for her "saltine crackers and tea" hospitality. I want to be that grandma.

Every Tuesday is officially Cousin Crew Playdate. We divide our grands by age into three groups for their special cousin time. While I can do a bit better than serving up a saltine lunch, it is the hospitality that counts.

For our grandchildren, this means paying attention, leaning in, listening to their small conversations, learning who they are as individuals in a family, and praying a blessing over them before they leave.

Isn't that always the goal of hospitality? Paying attention, listening, learning, and encouraging.

This week's kitchen island fare is homemade McD's: chicken nuggets, fries, and freezer applesauce. Next week's request is Berry French Toast.

Whether it be to neighbors, friends, or family, hospitality says, "I care. How are you?" There is a Bible verse on this subject. "Offer hospitality to one another without grumbling" (1 Peter 4:9 NIV).

Interestingly, this Scripture was written in the first century, where offering hospitality was extremely important for the survival of travelers such as letter carriers, pastors, teachers, and missionaries.

Today, we consider it a sacred honor. The rewards are sweet. I have a sleeve of saltines in my cupboard. Wanna come over?

I Reckon

It's winter, and I'm wide awake at 2 am. While I reach for my iced migraine bag, I hear the pitter-patter of rain hitting my windowpane. My mind switches seasons. We are in the full swing of a warm summer. I stay in the fun and sun for a few minutes and then pause because I know. I know it is wise to stay in the season.

Life runs on fast legs. The days are running faster and faster, and I can't afford to wish any of them away.

What do you do the week between Christmas and the New Year? I came across a century-old Irish tradition. Christmas bread was baked and then banged against the doors and walls while the women recited a prayer that would ensure them a plentiful year.

I can relate better to the Irish tradition of opening the new year with a clean house. Clearing away the added clutter and simplifying is my annual tradition, and it brings comfort to my space.

I find it more valuable each year. Also valuable is getting my heart in order: clearing out baggage I don't need to carry around, asking God's forgiveness when I've swerved off the path, and aligning my purpose to match His.

Wise Solomon told his sons the same thing his father, King David, advised him:

Above all else, guard your heart,
for everything you do flows from it.

(Proverbs 4:23 NIV)

Pay thoughtful attention.

The raindrops continue in the wee hours of the morning. Soon, I will resume clearing and cleaning, but only after I open God's pages. I aim to be ready for the New Year. My house and my heart.

Old Fangled

Some old-fashioned things like fresh air and sunshine
are hard to beat.

—Laura Ingalls Wilder

My windows at the inn are wide open, and my curtains sway in the breeze. The birds are singing their melodies. This morning, I feel a kindred spirit to Laura.

My mind drifts, and I wonder, "What could I do today that is old-fashioned?" (The irony does not escape me as I type this note on my laptop.)

Take a walk outside. Cook a meal to share with someone. Tend to my flowers. Visit with a neighbor. Talk to Jesus. Read His letter.

I can picture Laura opening her Bible to the prophet Jeremiah's words:

Stand at the crossroads and look;
ask for the ancient paths,
ask where the good way is, and walk in it,
and you will find rest for your souls.

(Jeremiah 6:16 NIV)

Crossroad: a turning point, a deciding moment. It is at a crossroad where we are all faced with making a decision.

Ancient path: God's people had lost their way time after time. The story of Israel is a long account of a nation that was willfully disobedient to God. Jeremiah was faithful in his calling. He pleaded with them to turn back to the Lord and take the path to peace where they would find rest for their souls.

Jeremiah's words still ring true for us today. Open God's Word, learn His truth, and walk in it.

It's a good trail. And a resting place for our hearts.

And now it's time for one more old-fashioned chore I share with Laura: cleaning the outhouse. I'm sending all my modern-day love to you, Laura.

What's on your old-fashioned list?

Pretense

Sharing our hearts is risky. Being vulnerable takes courage.

For those who don't know me personally, I am not an "out front" person. I shy away from being the center of attention. My comfortable spot is quietly taking up the back corner of a room. So how is it that I can greet and visit with people at church on our Guest Service Team and write publicly through social media?

I look for a common denominator. It's been a long time since math, but the dictionary says a common denominator is a feature shared by all.

I love connecting with people, and I am drawn to community. We need honest people who will pull away the mask of perfection. We need one another, people who get us.

I am an open book, and if you were to join me nook-side, I would share my struggles and failures with you. I can almost guarantee we all share something very difficult, a battle so overwhelming it grips us in heartache as we grope at an uphill climb. Our brokenness can lead us down the wrong path or to Jesus, the ultimate source of fulfilling our deepest needs.

We all have a story, and in our stories, there is brokenness. Thank you, Jesus, that you are the mender of hurting hearts. Thank you for piecing us together. We all need someone to say, "Come on, I'll listen. I'll share my imperfect, my broken pieces. We will find our way together."

I open my story pages to invite you to share yours.

Victory Cry!

The older I get, the more I appreciate daily rhythms and grounding habits. My simple formula for a good day is to read the Bible first, work out, and then do the most important or most difficult task on my to-do list before lunch.

As the calendar moves closer to spring, there is one annual rhythm that is my very favorite—Easter! Resurrection Sunday.

Of the many religions sincerely followed, only one is "won and done." Eternal life cannot be earned. Jesus paid it all. Because we cannot be good enough, He paid the sacrifice. And the best part of the story? As a child would say, "Jesus didn't stay dead."

Our grandson, who was with us for a few days, rehearsed the Easter story with me using our Resurrection Eggs (you can Google this wonderful object lesson if you aren't familiar with it—I'm still using my original homemade set from 1989). The eggs tell the story of the last days leading up to the crucifixion, and of course, the drama is set for that last egg to be opened, and our favorite moment arrives: the egg is empty!

We continued the same talk I shared with our children so long ago. If that tomb was not empty, we would have a dead Jesus. And a dead Jesus can't rescue us from our sin. If we have a dead Jesus, all the promises of the Bible are no good. All our prayers are no good. And our hope is no good. As long as Jesus is dead, nothing will be right with the world again.

But, oh, how wonderful it is! Plastic purple egg number twelve is empty. Jesus is alive! He has risen! Our promises, prayers, and hopes are alive. Jesus conquered death.

From the cross to the empty grave, Jesus won the day. And because of His win, I win this day! Peace in uncertainty. Hope in pain. My eternity is secured.

There will come a day when I'll no longer be with you. Do not worry or be sad for me—I will have made it Home.

My Kitchen View

Delicious autumn! My very soul is wedded to it, and if I were a bird, I would fly about the earth seeking the successive autumns.

—George Eliot, Letter to Miss Lewis

Unlike George, who is only wedded to autumn, I love all four seasons in Ohio. But our countryside is shouting pumpkins, and the leaves are drifting down at Wander Inn. It is time to slip quietly into our lovely "fall and spice" and make everything nice.

Do you have a favorite season? Mine, without hesitancy, is the next one. Usually, I'm ready to move forward, tiring after a bit of too much heat, then too much cold, then too much rain.

An air of expectancy in the next season draws me in. Apart from house decorating, the calendar informs our home routines and my kitchen menu.

Wouldn't it be crummy to be stuck in just one season? And yet, maybe you are. Today I heard the voice of disappointment of a match not made—oh, the hard dating years. Another voice, a friend stuck in declining health with no good prognosis on the horizon. Yet another heartache so deep words cannot express.

Waiting. Deferred hope. Pain. Mourning. Too hard. Too long. Too difficult.

I've had my share of "fed-ups" with parts of my current season, making me ready to move on to the next. If you're still reading, maybe you are too.

But here is what I know as I lean forward. There are lessons yet to be gleaned in this right now season. And here is mine: contentment—the sweet, inward, quiet, gracious spirit that freely accepts and delights in God's wise plan.

Seasons don't last forever. And even in the most difficult of circumstances, we are held. "My times are in your hands" (Psalm 31:15 NIV). Jesus will always be our refuge.

This autumn I'm working on this character trait of mine. It simply will not do to bake pumpkin pies with a discontented soul.

Happy, a Hack, and a Habit

I did something new. With my Bible, book, planner, and coffee, I switched seats.

I moved from my nook to our great room. (Is that what they still call it? Great things do happen in our open living room/kitchen, but I need a better name. *Great room* seems a bit stuffy for cottage life.) I digress.

It's interesting what a change of scenery does for perspective. I think it is why vacations were invented.

So I'm writing from my whatever room, trying not to notice the meal halfway prepped for the next hour. What I do notice are the love seats and chairs, and they are not sad.

Yesterday I had three gals over to talk about the Bible. It was a delightful time welcoming them into our whatever room. Over our discussion about Jesus, with coffee, tea, and cream puff cake, I made a new friend. Nothing warms my heart faster.

Hospitality is a simple plan to say welcome. A lit candle and antique plates bought many years ago from a thrift store held a sweet dessert. It need not be fancy.

One small touch I like to add is changing paper napkins according to seasons or whimsy. (Cloth napkins that need to be ironed have not yet married with casual cottage life. Don't hold your breath waiting!)

I like to buy pretty paper napkins when I see them marked on clearance. As I pulled out this beautiful blue-and-brown thick plaid napkin, an idea popped into my head. Grab scissors and cut on the seam. In seconds, I doubled the number of plaid guest napkins from sixteen to thirty-two. Not one lady noticed they were using only half a napkin. Whatever room smiles.

I know this is a very small hack (it seems one could have invented a lovelier name for good ideas!), and it won't change the world's ills. But it did charm a certain innkeeper's heart.

And if you have time for one more simple idea, curtains for your kitchen window. Buy a tension rod and hanging clips. There are many pretty seasonal kitchen towels to choose from. No ironing is necessary, and they're easy on the budget. Cut off the tags and hang the dish towels. Instant decor that is charming, inn or no inn.

It is always good to shift scenery, even if only in a 1,840-square-foot inn.

What's in a Name?

My name is Margi Jo Deeks. It is not the same as what is written on my birth certificate, Marjorie Joan Mayo. Mom named me after her two friends, both pastors' wives. Although my full name was never used, it is my signature.

I had an easy time choosing my new title before our first grandchild was born. It made perfect sense. The *gi* at the end of Margi became Gigi.

I still smile over my Gigi name; hearing it hundreds of times never gets old—only I do! As my grandchildren grow older, I'm often answering to Gig.

I worked in the customer service department for three years at Elyria Phone Company. All of our work was represented by initials (this was back in the day before computers), and our work was signed by hand. When I was offered the job, there was a stipulation—I needed to choose a different phone name. To avoid confusion with similar initials as mine, I became Tara Lee.

As a side note, forty years later, I found Tara Leigh Cobble, an excellent online Bible teacher. I smile when I hear her name.

I have had my share of new names, but the best is my "knew" name. Knowing I am known turns my world upside down, or better yet, right side up.

One of my favorite verses in the Bible says this:

Fear not, for I have redeemed you.
I have called you by your name, you are mine.

(Isaiah 43:1 ESV)

Of the billions of people we share a planet with, not many know my name. In the big scheme of things, I'm not all that important, except to One.

Imagine being personally known by the God of the universe. He names me as His own. He loves me. He chose me. He sent His Son, Jesus, to die for me. He delights in me, and He sings over me. He calls my name.

Today, His call carries me to write and grocery shop.

Signed, Marjorie Joan Mayo, Tara Lee, Margi Deeks, Gigi, and best of all, child of God.

Sandals and Ice Pops

Summer. It's the season of unhurried long days and late nights, birds singing, rain showers, and chocolate ice cream.

I want to remember day trips, vacations, bonding with old friends and forging new friendships, porch parties, family togetherness, and new serving privileges. This makes a happy summer.

> Stan Hywet Hall and Gardens, OH. Rated: most interesting.
> Brandywine Falls, OH. Rated: most breathtaking.
> Donut Shop, Geneva on the Lake. Rated: most yum.
> Camp Patmos, Kelleys Island. Rated: most heavenly.
> Cleveland Blues Cruise. Rated: most unique.
> Our Cabin, PA. Rated: most inspiring.
> Cleveland Museum of Art. Rated: most culture.
> Neighborhood block party. Rated: most important.

The steps of summer—how I want them to linger. Lazy days to drink deeply from the ancient truths. As my cute water bottle helps refresh me, I'm reminded that the Bible is not an academic book. It is living, powerful, and life-changing. Read it and pray through it.

The law of the Lord is perfect (flawless),
restoring and refreshing the soul;
The statutes of the Lord are reliable and trustworthy,
making wise the simple.
The precepts of the Lord are right, bringing joy to the heart;
The commandment of the Lord is pure, enlightening the eyes.

(Psalm 19:7–8 AMP)

And that rating: most precious.

47 Years of Friendship

I meant to do my work today—
But a brown bird sang in the apple tree,
And a butterfly flitted across a field,
And all the leaves were calling me.

—Richard Le Gallienne

My husband and I travel across Pennsylvania to visit my college friend and see their lovely new home and tree-lined acreage. Although I don't spy any apple trees, they do have a stunning view of the mountains.

Over many cups of shared coffee, our friendship travels back to 1977, when we were dormmates. There are never enough hours for catch-up conversations. Blessings we recount on one hand. On the other, deep sorrows. Friends and family are going through what I can only describe as traumatic. We pause and pray.

God reminds us that we are held—not 53 percent held but 100 percent. This is not a pie-in-the-sky kind of hope but one anchored in Jesus, who walked to the cross for us and now walks through the storms with us. Jesus is our anchor, our Savior, our ever-flowing fountain of hope. He never runs dry, even when we do.

The days spent in the company of dear friends are soul-refreshing. Another cup of coffee to do nothing but chat away the hours. Grace-fueled. Hearts refreshed—a quiet composure.

I would share the lovely mountain view with you today from our friend's back deck if I could. Instead, I will have to settle for sharing my heart's view. It comes with coffee.

12 Months to Practice

The new year is still fresh, and I'm tiptoeing in. I am in the habit of choosing a theme word for the new year rather than making resolutions. Out of the three words that bounce around in my head, the word that finally lands is *worship*.

What is worship? Our response to God for who He is and what He's done . . . expressed in what we say and the way we live.

Seems like a very large word for ordinary ole me. But since this word seems to have chosen me, I'm determined to unpack it in practical terms. Here's a start. Worship is my gift to God.

God has done so much for me. It would fill pages to recount. My response? Use my words to praise Him and give Him back my time and abilities.

I believe God has uniquely gifted each of us. Our aptitudes and natural abilities are all different. Imagine waking each morning and asking God, "What gift can I give you today?"

Worship might involve baking to take, sending a card, giving away ten or fifty dollars, organizing a playroom for little people, sharing what Jesus has done, prayer walking . . . an endless list.

> *Through Jesus, therefore, let us continually offer to God a sacrifice of praise—the fruit of lips that openly profess his name. And do not forget to do good and to share with others, for with such sacrifices God is pleased.*

(Hebrews 13:15–16 NIV)

In my sacred place, offer to Jesus what costs me something.

There is great comfort in unpacking a newish year together. Or, as Winnie-the-Pooh says, "A day without a friend is like a pot without a single drop of honey left inside."[2]

Together, we fill honey pots. I count it as worship.

Don't Get Stuck on a Stump

I read about two bald eagles at the Tampa zoo who were permanently injured. The pair of beautiful kings of the sky were grounded. Because they could no longer soar, no covering was needed over their habitat. They were often photographed settled on a stump.

Not able to get this sad plight of the eagles out of my mind, I asked myself, "Am I soaring? Or am I settling for life on a stump?"

Sometimes life serves up good reasons to settle for stump living. Circumstances that are impossible to manage, difficulties that hang around . . . you can fill in the blank.

What do grounded eagles do when they can't fly away on vacation? When they can't escape unchanging realities? Eagles can create. (I'm an eagle.)

Enter my flannelgraph project—one trip to Walmart. Purchase a large mailer box and flannel. Work with hubby, a bonus! Cut and staple. And there you have a lightweight flannelgraph board for storytelling.

And what stories might Gigi tell her eleven young grandchildren?

- Let's not panic with Henny Penny: the sky is a-falling.
- Three little pigs prove hard work does pay off.
- And a favorite Bible story, a woman and a well.

The woman, living in shame, was a social outcast, demeaned, and disregarded. She had five husbands and a live-in.

The woman met someone who could unstick her from her slump, or stump. Jesus, the Living Water.

The One who promises, "Those who hope in the Lord will renew their strength. They will soar on wings like eagles; they will run and not grow weary; they will walk and not be faint" (Isaiah 40:31 NIV).

Circumstances don't dictate us to a life lived on a stump. The woman at the well soared after her encounter with Jesus. She had a "chance" meeting while drawing water at the well. She was curious enough to ask questions about life.

Her story is a rich example of love, truth, redemption, and acceptance, and it had a happy ending.

Who knew an eagle was soaring in my neighborhood? She's been spotted at the inn, wearing lipstick.

Innkeeper's Diary

Six days in my recliner. Six most unproductive days—no innkeeping and no spring decorating.

I miss the two unusually warm days for winter in Ohio. My daily core training halts abruptly while Augmentin, prednisone, and prescribed cough syrup keep me company along with a majority of useless TV consumption.

Through the crummiest of days, it does not escape me. Yes, I am sick. But it isn't cancer, as some of my dear friends are battling. It's not a tragic course that others are facing. It's just a very temporary setback.

Is there a lesson in my story this day? I wish I could say I suffer well, but I don't. I'm impatient with pain. I'm not a fan of hours that creep by, the night hours being the hardest. The neck nerves go haywire, adding to the other fun symptoms. I longingly watch for normal to return.

I listen to praise music as I seek the silver lining. And I hear a strain that mentions someone is praying for you.

My spirit is bolstered by this reminder. And my heart is challenged. I can be the someone. My most unproductive days can be filled with lasting productivity—praying for others, even while feeling crummy. The list is long. On the top today, a dear family lost a father to cancer and, in the same week, their beloved dog. So, lazing away in my recliner, I lift this family to the Throne.

On the evening of my epiphany comes a ding, a Marco Polo from our two-year-old grandson with a birthday request: can we buy him a boat to play with in the bathtub?

As it turns out, I have found two productive things I can do while in sick bay: pray and Amazon. Both bring a smile as I reach for another pill.

Slam Dunk

My husband and I like to watch the NBA playoff series. Because we don't have streaming channels, we watch the next day on YouTube. Before we know it, watching the speed game highlight reel, we are in the fourth quarter, at the end of the game.

It is much like us in life. My husband and I are both of Medicare age. We are in our fourth quarter of life. For anyone who knows the game of basketball, the fourth quarter is not the time to slack off. We want to finish well.

I was reminded of this challenge: do what matters most. The only way to find the answer to this is to open God's conversation with us—the Bible. God will show us. It is His design to be our Guide.

There is a lot that matters, right? Hello, clean clothes and food on the table. But what matters most? Jesus said it best: "Follow me."

If you're new to the Bible and want to start learning, try the Gospel of Luke. The author, Dr. Luke, narrated Jesus' birth, ministry, death, and resurrection. Soak in Jesus' fascinating life and teaching. You just may be surprised.

It's my passion to connect people to Jesus and the Living Word. I pray you will open God's love letter to you if you aren't already in the habit. It is an invitation that changes a life.

Meanwhile, back to the least of all that matters: basketball.

Quiet Arrives

Something new. In thirty-eight years, my Christmas tree has seen red and white, gold, turquoise and silver, country, and classic traditional decor. Our first year in our rehabbed home, we bought a new tree with what looked like thousands of tiny white lights. It was so pretty that I left it un-ornamented, to the displeasure of my older grand girls.

As is my custom, I decorate for winter and then add minimal Christmas decor. This year, I decide to quiet the season by adding a touch of color to the tree. I bring you a new color. We are dressed in pink! Enchantment at the inn is accomplished. And without knowing it, merchandisers apparently felt that same need. There is a lot of blush pink out there just waiting to break from tradition.

There is quiet in my nook this morning. Carols are playing while I write by the fire, accompanied by my balsam candle aroma.

Can I find a Scripture that ties in to my pink theme? I'm glad you asked, and yes!

In quietness and confidence is your strength.

(Isaiah 30:15 NLT)

The word for *quietness* in Hebrew is *shaqat* (shaw-kat'). It means calm, undisturbed, free from anxiety. Tranquil. Serene.

Pink does not mad dash about in a frenzy of activity, rushing from one pursuit to another. Instead, it has a heart that pauses, focuses clearly, and surrenders all the good and hard pieces of a little life to God.

As the calendar page turns to December, where lovely reds and greens greet us at every turn, pink and I will hold our place.

And a postscript—in case you're wondering how hubs feels about my color choice, here's his one word: elegant. The carpenter that I married has good taste.

In Every Life, a Birthday Must Fall

*To keep the heart unwrinkled, to be hopeful, kindly, cheerful,
reverent—that is to
triumph over old age.*

—Thomas Bailey Aldrich

Turning sixty-five was a cheery occasion with many lovely greetings and special surprises. The sweetest surprise came from my grandchildren, who sang "Happy Birthday" to me in French! The same grands who guessed me to be about thirty-nine. Gigi smiles. *Bonne fête to me.*

I want to memorize the moments.

Getting ready while on vacation, my five-year-old granddaughter joined me in the bathroom. She sorted through my makeup bag and, holding up a tube, promptly asked, "Gigi, is this the one that helps fill in the cracks on your face?" Gigi smiles.

Every day, I'm presented with a fresh opportunity to make good choices and live life well. The book of Proverbs in the Bible has great wisdom in guiding a life:

> *Trust in the Lord with all your heart*
> *and lean not on your own understanding;*
> *in all your ways submit to him*
> *and he will make your paths straight.*

(Proverbs 3:5–6 NIV)

I wonder if this is what Thomas Bailey Aldrich meant by keeping a heart unwrinkled: live a trusting life and follow Jesus as your guide.

I'm all in. I am especially considering the antonyms for *unwrinkled*: rumpled, bumpy, and ruffled.

It all depends on the day.

Rest Stop

A favorite memory in our family growing up was loading the big van and heading to our cousins' dairy farm in Cement City, Michigan. Only three hours away from home, the days held the kind of fun we didn't have on Capel Road: milking cows, making forts in the tall stacked hay bales, and walking to the nickel candy store. We celebrated each summer with softball games, tractor rides, and home-cranked ice cream.

En route to our destiny, I can still remember this oft-asked question: "When is the next rest stop?" Finding a roadside facility with restrooms was essential on a road trip.

And it still is. We need a rest, a stop built into our days. How long until the next rest stop?

It can be found between two deep breaths.

Jesus offered this invitation: "Come to me, all of you who are weary and carry heavy burdens, and I will give you rest" (Matthew 11:28 NLT).

Try this breath prayer:

- Inhale: You made me and sustain me.
- Exhale: You carry me all of my days.
- Repeat.

Gone are the idyllic farm days of my youth, when I seemingly had few cares or worries. Somehow, in the years that piled up, life got complicated. But God has given us an internal compass that draws us to a resting place.

Today it's not a hay bale I'm looking for but the next rest stop around the bend. I'm RSVPing to Jesus' invite to a fixed and permanent place to land. Come weary or worn, ragged or torn.

Refined by the Shore

One of the wonderful benefits of our annual summer pilgrimage by ferry to Kelleys Island is my walk along the shore of Lake Erie.

Having always been an early morning riser, just like my dad, the 4:30 alarm rings. Before all the fun, noise, and chaos of our eleven grandchildren waking on the grounds of our beloved Camp Patmos, I am on a quiet stroll.

I lean in, listening. Waves lapping, birds singing, I hear God's whisper.

Some of my most significant life adjustments have been made along that shore. Brisk energy for a flagging spirit. Finding a deeper friendship with Jesus. Renewed hope in a time of intense anxiety. I have learned over and over that God is bigger than I thought.

Our church theme is "Living the adventure of becoming like Christ." My adventure began when I accepted Jesus as my Savior when I was five. Following Jesus has been an exciting journey.

I rehearse His blessings as I walk the familiar worn steps along the Lake Erie shore, a walk I've been familiar with since I was a third-grade camper. I look up. The oldest of our grands, age nine, runs out to join my walk, reminding me again that God has been so very good to me. And I say a quiet prayer that all eleven grandchildren will have their own exciting adventure of walking with Jesus.

Let all that I am praise the Lord;
with my whole heart I will praise his holy name.
Let all that I am praise the Lord;
may I never forget the good things he does for me.

(Psalm 103:1–2 NLT)

The bone-weariness after five days of nonstop Camp Patmos activity? It's proof positive that I'm not that same nine-year-old girl excitedly running all over the camp fifty-six years ago. But here is what is precious to me—that nine-year-old girl could never have guessed how greatly God would use twenty-seven acres and a chapel to help chart the course of her life.

Thank you, Lord, for preserving this land on Kelleys Island called Camp Patmos that serves as a *"A Light to All Generations."*

Mirror, Mirror on the Wall

I spent a few hours in the presence of a lovely elderly lady. Other than hearing of her struggle with a neurological disease, not once did I hear her mention any struggle with beauty issues. What did she glow about? Her Bible club work in a city school, a recent trip to a third-world country where she fed those with HIV/AIDS, and a week of vacation helping disabled children at a summer camp.

It was refreshing to be in her company. I admired her. She possessed a rare quality—a beauty that can't be purchased, a beauty that counts for eternity. It is what I seek.

We live in an obsessed world that defines our worth by our appearance. The plethora of products on the market is proof of the quest to slow down the aging process. We receive the world's labels, trying to become more of this or less of that, and trade the truth of who we are in God's eyes for a lie.

I hold a beauty manual, God's Word, which has something valuable to add to the conversation and offers the best clothing apparel.

Therefore, as God's chosen people, holy and dearly loved,
clothe yourselves with compassion, kindness, humility,
gentleness and patience.

(Colossians 3:12 NIV)

And then this description, found in the Book of Wisdom, fits my elderly friend well:

Charm is deceptive, and beauty is fleeting,
but a woman who fears the Lord is to be praised.

(Proverbs 31:30 NIV)

I have written in the margin of my Bible, "Because you love me, Jesus, I am lovely." May that theme beat deep into our hearts. I want to be that woman with a light in my eyes, a glow on my face, and warmth in my words—unfading beauty.

And I do think you might find her bathroom counter is graced with various shades of pink lipstick.

Curating a File

I have been asked, "What's on your bucket list?" What do you want to experience before you kick the bucket?

I would like to include a few places on that list: road-tripping out west, cruising up the East Coast, taking in the beautiful Grand Canyon, and touring Israel with our pastor. Unfortunately, with my neck issues worsening each year, the probability of checking these off diminishes.

I am learning to accept my limitations. When life doesn't go according to plan, I make a different bucket list. It may not consist of sizeable adventures, but it carries a great weight of importance.

Louisa May Alcott, at age thirteen, wrote, "How can I keep a sunny soul / To shine along life's way? How can I tune my little heart / To sweetly sing all day?"[3]

I am getting better at finding beauty and adventure in my own backyard. Each new season I create a Cousin Crew adventure list that is written on our kitchen chalkboard.

Spending time under the redwoods along the coast of California sounds wondrous. I would love to spend a week in Ireland, checking out dear old bookshops and out-of-the-way tea shops and walking wild and windy paths.

It takes a measure of planning to travel around the world, but it takes great courage to tent camp with eleven grandchildren.

Perhaps a smaller life was my meant life. And oddly enough, I'm okay with that.

Measuring Cup

I have a beautiful white pitcher on my kitchen island with the phrase "Always half full" imprinted on it. I need the daily reminder.

I'm cozied up with my blanket and coffee in our nook, thinking about the word *limitations*. The word itself doesn't sound pleasant. It sounds a lot like restriction. To curb, to impede.

Like most of us, aside from spiritual blessings, we don't have unlimited resources, unlimited energy, or unlimited . . . (you fill in the blank).

When it comes right down to it, I don't want a limiting life. I doubt you do, either. I want a liberating life. Freedom. I don't want medical or any other issues to determine my calendar.

This thought pressed in as I woke to another less-than day with my neck issues. What if my limitations are actually a gift from God's hand?

While I'm still working this out, here is what I know: suffering is universal. It's a constant we all experience living in a fallen, broken world. But how we respond in the face of suffering determines the track of our lives.

When I'm fully whole and on the go, I don't need God nearly as much. My deficits and neediness give me a front-row seat to witness God's beautiful divine work.

And that witness helps one more time. Bear what comes with grace. We can, together.

With my second cup of coffee in hand, I share my morning song: "The Lord is my portion; therefore, I will wait for him." (Lamentations 3:24 NIV).

May our cups overflow.

Drop the Mic

This week I watched an interesting video in which a famous business magnate was asked, "Do you know the meaning of life?"

I was curious to hear the answer from someone highly intelligent, ambitious, and successful.

His response was interesting. "Go out there and expand consciousness. We can't really answer that question yet. How do molecules have thoughts and emotions?"

I give the gentleman credit for his honesty and curiosity. Asking questions is a good place to begin.

I prayed for this wildly successful, wealthy man, that his quest would lead him not to AI (artificial intelligence) for the answers but to Jesus—his Creator, Designer, and who I hoped would someday become his Redeemer.

On this beautiful sunny day with green trees and vibrant-colored birds, I pause and give thanks. Ordinary people like me, with fewer brains, less fame, and less means, can know the answer to that interview question with certainty.

Ask yourself, "What is the meaning of life? What is truly important?" Then build your life around the answer. (Hint: the Bible provides the answer.)

Mic handoff, this is my answer: to know God, enjoy God, share God, and reflect some of His beauty. It's a good place to start.

Wordsmith

Several times a year, the longing arises to declutter our inn's closets, drawers, pantry, and vanities. It seems there is either too much stuff or not enough storage. My attempt at minimizing keeps me vigilant.

In all my sorting, clearing, and storing, if wishes were reality, I would own a spacious carriage house like the one we previously owned. Oh, did you not know we have a carriage house, albeit a narrow one? In modern-day terms, it is our garage.

My mind meanders—from carriage houses to couches. I remember sharing with my grandchildren some different names for the simple couches they sat on. A settee, divan, sofa. I added my favorite word, *davenport*. Merriam-Webster says it can also mean a small, compact writing desk.

Did you grow up with a davenport in your house? I did, and I still think it's a funny word. Upon researching, I found the word was first recorded in 1853, right alongside *brain fog*.

I'm grateful that I own both a carriage house and a davenport. And I'm happy to declare there is not a brain fog in sight, yet. Hold on. The day is new.

Wander Inn Declutter is almost checked off. Three more closets this week are on my agenda. The carriage house is on the hub's checklist. The house is quieting. And I am cheerful.

Time for coffee on the davenport. I wish you could join me.

Holding a Hand

A picture of our newborn grandson bedded in a baby hospital bed popped up in my photo memories. I had to pause and reflect momentarily on the miracle we were given.

The gravity of our newborn's health was written in the photo on his mama's face. As our little world felt like it was collapsing, our little one was surrounded by love and prayer warriors. And in God's mercy, bacterial meningitis did not become part of his story.

Our praises never end, but I can't help but think about all the miracles pleaded for that remain unanswered. Do I have an answer for that? Why do bad things happen to good people?

I don't have an answer that will take away the pain, the hurt, the awful devastation. I wonder if we could ask Jesus, "Do you have an answer?"

I imagine the words might come quietly: "I hate death, pain, and suffering. They are now part of life, far from my original design of beauty. Sin destroys. But the greatest miracle was that I came to redeem all the darkness. There is a bigger picture than what you can see now. Take my hand, and I'll walk you through the turbulence. Let my perfect peace calm you in every circumstance and give you courage and strength for every challenge."

What Jesus did say is recorded in John 14:1: "Let not your hearts be troubled . . . believe also in me" (ESV). While sighing and sorrow are part of life on this side of eternity, it won't always be this way.

Oh, my friend, who may be struggling right now, I am writing to you today. My hand holds yours. You have two companions. One resides at Wander Inn, and the other, Jesus, was turned away from an inn.

May Jesus' journey to the manger and the cross and from the empty tomb give us a brave walk this day. And just maybe we will find a sprinkling of joy mixed with hope.

RSVP

Have you ever been invited to tea and crumpets?

Tea and crumpets do sound like a lovely combination, except I'm more of a coffee sipper, and I've never eaten a crumpet. So I researched the subject. Hailing from England, I found they are a cross between an English muffin and a pancake. (It seems to me they should have added more sugar into that recipe!)

Back to my invitation.

You are cordially invited to tea and crumpets at Wander Inn Cottage. But be forewarned:

1. I don't own a proper tea service.
2. I have two tea selections: peppermint and Red Rose.
3. In my attempt to watch carbs, can I offer you tea with a hard-boiled egg?

If you're still willing to accept my invitation, might I make an additional offer? Coffee and conversation cozied up fireside. Ah, and what might we talk about? World problems, soup recipes, TV screen cleaning, carbs in hard-boiled eggs, and Jesus.

I hope Jesus always gets our attention. Tea or coffee, His invitation is always open. Over 2,000 years ago, Jesus stood and said, "Anyone who is thirsty may come to me!" (John 7:37 NLT).

It's an invitation worth your RSVP.

Candles and Truth

This phrase ran through my mind as I emptied my white-and-gray hutch, which houses all my candles: "To thine own self be true."[4]

In my pursuit of living big in a smaller home, I made a pact to burn the candles I already had before purchasing more. As I pulled out my candles, I organized them in seasons. It looked as though my budget would be happy until next fall.

I'm not much into Shakespeare's *Hamlet*, where that phrase originated. "I just need to be true to myself." That is a good intention, but I wonder if there is a cautionary note about it.

The word *true*. Today our world would have us define *truth* as whatever floats our boats, whatever is trending, making up our truth according to our desires. The truth today is being determined by what is preferred and what is popular.

I stop for a moment of reflection. Do these beliefs align with God's truth?

I believe God is Truth, and He has given us absolutes found in the Bible. And therein lies the beauty. God is our personal Designer. His truth is not meant to cage us in or limit us. It is in God's truth we find the freedom to operate in the most beautiful way possible.

It is God's truth, not our desires, that points the way to freedom: "You will know the truth, and the truth will set you free" (John 8:32 ESV).

We are back where we started. With my fresh cuppa, I'm about to light my lovely candle gifted from a friend who doesn't know about my secret candle pact. I'm keeping my part of "to thine own self be true."

Inserting a grateful smile for the candle gift.

Stretched Faith

Last week was bad—bad enough that I experienced a faith storm for three days. It was another horrible vomiting-pain migraine episode, one of many I've experienced for over twenty years. I am sure that in your own troubled and challenging times, your conversation with God might sound a lot like mine:

God, I know you can.

God, I know you care.

But, God, will you come?

Later I penned those words in my journal, followed by this statement: "When you don't feel His presence, and everything is agonizingly silent, you believe He is there. And faith grows in the disappointment and pain."

The journal page closed.

Until four days later, when God said, "Not so fast. Who told you to put a period on your request?"

It would take pages to recount the miracle God gave me. A prayer I agonized over for nine years was answered. And on a very ordinary Sunday morning, my eyes beheld. Our prodigal came full circle.

And God did come. Beautifully, surprisingly, abundantly.

Be careful where you place those periods.

82° and Sunny

This was the weather caption in the days leading up to our first annual campout. Our kids asked all week, "Gigi, are we going to get rain?"

"Eighty-two degrees and sunny," said the weatherman daily.

It was a sunny start to our first fun Friday campout. We pitched three tents in our son's backyard. Two hours later, black clouds rolled in, and rain fell.

"It will be a quick shower," Gigi said.

"Everyone indoors," Gigi said.

The rain came harder. And it lasted longer.

While enjoying the cozy indoor cousin play, phone alerts sounded the alarm.

"Tornado warning for our county," alerted the local weatherman.

82° and sunny.

S'mores were eaten by a propane camp stove, under dripping umbrellas. Sleeping bags moved from campout to camp-in. Thunder, lightning, and rain throughout the night. And the cousins could not have had more fun.

When life hands you 82° and sunny, make what? As if the menu knew, our daughter-in-law served a pitcher of fresh-squeezed lemonade along with the rain—sweetness in abundance.

In the next long, hard rainstorm, Gigi will be smiling: 82° and sunny. It seems to go with tent camping.

Girl Meets Boy

The magical date is April 6, 1985. Happy anniversary to my hubby and best friend. I know it sounds sappy, but if I had to choose again, I would always and forever choose you.

It's been said to marry a man who sings to you. I smile. How about marrying a man who can build for you? And wow, have we built! You have given me two beautiful homes. As much as I have loved my nests, the best thing we have built together is our family and our lifework.

As a freshman in high school, I could never have known I would be watching my future husband play for the opposing basketball team. Who would have known we shared a space for three years of basketball games? If you had looked up in the stands, you would have seen a quiet girl cheering. You couldn't have known she would be the one you would propose to.

The boy and girl went to college. The boy played sports and became a teacher, while the girl played no sports, became a surgical assistant technician, and dreamed of babies.

Then, in 1984, life shifted. The boy bought a fixer-upper house next door to the girl, and a beautiful love story began. A year later, after the first racquetball date, a life verse and wedding rings were chosen.

The Lord has done great things for us,
And we are glad.

(Psalm 126:3 NKJV)

The years are rolling by too fast. What joy it is to look back at all God has done for us. Our marriage has worked because Jesus is our best friend. As we walk hand in hand through these latter years, what peace to know that our future is secure. One day we will be separated, but it will only be temporary because our love story is built on Jesus' love story.

The girl got more than she ever dreamed, even an off-key melody heard at the inn.

Choose Well

Due to my lack of a green thumb and a sunny windowsill, I don't do well with live plants. For a couple of dollars, I often pick up fresh herbs that add green life to my countertop and are useful in my cooking.

The sweet potted herb serves as a good reminder. (1) There is another way, and (2) no matter the circumstances, strive for perspective.

Let's peek beyond the view of green plants. Is it possible to have happiness in dire situations? Is it a stretch? It depends on our definition of *happiness*.

Yesterday I was on my third day of a cluster neck-nerve, and being happy would *not* have described my mood of the day.

George Müller, a missionary born in 1805, helped care for over 10,000 orphans in Bristol, England. He was thoroughly acquainted with hardship and uncertainty, and the challenges he faced increased his faith and trust. His stories still influence many today, including me.

The first great and primary business to which I ought to attend
every day was, to have my soul happy in the Lord.

—George Müller[5]

Choose ahead of time. Come what may this day, God has portioned out for me just what I need. Joys, sorrow, pain, productivity.

A focus. A frame of mind. My real treasure is Jesus. Trust Him. Choose Him.

For I, the Lord your God,
hold your right hand (unbelievable when you think on it!);
it is I who say to you, "Fear not,
I am the one who helps you."

(Isaiah 41:13 ESV, parenthesis added)

Oh, friends, we can be conductors of happiness. Our role does not eliminate despairing circumstances and hard places. But it does provide needed perspective. God's wooing grace covers.

You find what you seek. My small green pot of rosemary concurs.

Productive Rest

Is that an oxymoron? Two words that seemingly contradict each other. In my world this week, these two words are sitting side by side. It's kind of like hubby and me—alone together. (Are you catching an oxymoron theme here?)

We are spending a cottage week in Huron, just thirty-three miles from home. We trek out for a daily walk along the shores of our beloved Lake Erie. We catch both sunrises and sunsets.

At the end of the week, our kiddos and grands join us for beach fun. Did I hear you add another oxymoron? Organized chaos.

On our agenda: annual matching pajamas, crocheted beddies for teddy bears, papa's homemade wooden beds for kitties and our first official family kickball game.

Until the noise arrives, we soak in a less hurried pace on a lovely covered patio. With our Bibles and notebooks, we pray, dream, and create.

To go as I am led, to go when I am led, to go where I am led; it is
that which has been for twenty years the one prayer of my life.

—Arthur Pierson[6]

A listening prayer pulls up a seat next to productive rest.

Oxymorons are done. Awfully good that you let me share with you.

Finding the Key

The last four days were spent in my pajamas. After a few miserable flu days, a mind shift was needed.

I powered up the news to see how our world was faring in my absence. Each story brought unbearable and unthinkable sound bites. A mind shift was needed.

I got a phone call from a loved one. My heart tumbled. A mind shift was needed.

Thanksgiving week arrived. Is there a better way to shift a mind than to put it into a thankful gear?

The list of troubles is long, and the list of unfixables is longer. But the longest list is a wonderful, beautiful, generous list of blessings! A mind shift settled in.

As I counted my place settings to serve twenty-six at our Thanksgiving table, I counted my blessings. And what makes number one at the top of my list? Jesus. Because to shift my mind, He had to shift my heart.

We need more than just a positive spin. We need a positive reality: Jesus and the boundless riches of His gospel grace. He already did what we could never do for ourselves on the cross.

If you welcome a mind shift but are a little fuzzy on what a Jesus heart shift looks like. Find me. I'll be buried under my to-do list, but I love two things: sharing Jesus and setting up three tablescapes.

Refreshed

What dreadful hot weather we have! It keeps one in a continual state of inelegance.

—Jane Austen

Iced coffee. The best I can do in my lovely glass-etched mug is add coffee and cream and place it in the refrigerator to cool. It's not the taste of Starbucks, but it's refreshing in this last heat wave of our summer.

I slurp my iced beverage and recall something I heard years ago from an old-time preacher: saints are not carried to heaven on couches.

Did he mean to imply that air-conditioning is not essential to life?

Who knew my husband (who suffers from chronic sinus issues; therefore, our AC only runs when we have company) has much in common with Mr. Old-Time Preacher? I smile.

Meanwhile, there are two more days of inelegance. Be strong, I tell myself, on the battlefield, under the fans.

If your battle reaches beyond the thermometer, here is a bolstering quote from God's Word:

> *Have I not commanded you? Be strong and courageous. Do not be frightened, and do not be dismayed, for the Lord your God is with you wherever you go.*
>
> (Joshua 1:9 ESV)

Take heart. Find a friend who will listen. A shared burden is one cut in half. Then find another friend who is running her AC.

The Power of the Little Inch

What can one little inch do today, assuming the inch is moving? Let me count the ways:

- Locate condiments in the refrigerator, the same fridge that has not gotten the memo: a place for everything and everything in its place. Mustard wanders to the dairy shelf, and salad dressings prefer orange juice as their BFF.
- Lace up walking shoes.
- Bake a new dessert. Try not to eat the new dessert.
- Make that phone call.
- Wash the summer throw.
- Reach for the cookie, which turns into reaching for the ice cream, which turns into waiting 'til Monday to begin a new diet.

The little inch can carry us forward or backward. Let's vote—forward!

Have you heard this? Our decisions determine our direction, and our direction determines our destiny.

The decisions we make with our inch today determine the stories we tell tomorrow. It matters. The little decisions we make every day are of infinite importance. I need the reminder.

My power inch reaches for morning coffee with my spinach omelet. For the record, I still struggle with my food reach—I think I always will—but I'm toting along my inch of optimism.

How is your little inch doing?

If you are faithful in little things,
you will be faithful in large ones.

(Luke 16:10 NLT)

I'm holding the banner for us. Advance, little inch!

Muddle Fuddle

We enjoy a wonderful family vacation at a cottage located in Huron, Ohio, just an hour's drive from home. (This vacation has been gifted to us for several years, yet another of God's blessings!) We relax in our quiet times until the weekend, then Joyful Noise arrives. Our entire family lands for beautiful hours of togetherness.

In the midst of this vacation, I receive a text from one of our Oberlin Conservatory friends asking if they can spend the night with us before their dorm opens. (We offer our home to college kids needing a home away from home, occasionally filling them up with pizza and salad.) Of course, I responded with a yes.

Returning from our getaway week, I hit the ground running. You know the post-vacation feeling of exhaustion. As I prep an easy breakfast and quickly clean through the house, I am reminded how blessed I am to have a space to offer.

Want a peek into my messy, still-learning heart? Our previous home was set up beautifully for guests. No tiptoeing was needed—plenty of spacious bathrooms and master suites, all on a separate floor for guests.

The way Wander Inn (our current home) is arranged—two small bedrooms and a playroom share a short hallway and our only full bathroom. Whispering is required. The two college gals don't seem to mind. The friend who chose the single bed shares her sleep with trucks and dollies.

Serving up my potato sausage casserole with a side of blueberries and zucchini bread, I remember why we said "yes." We are privileged to hear the hearts of two nineteen-year-old, hard-working, intelligent gals. What a joy to pray with them before they stand in the registration line of their junior year.

Waving a see you later, I head for laundry detail, and my eyes catch sight of our dollhouse. A bit discombobulated! Far from perfect. I smile. It's okay. We offer what we have to give.

I'm reminded again of that principle that whoever refreshes others will be refreshed.

That give always bounces back. Lovely college gals, harpist and hornist, you are exactly what God prescribed for this muddled, fuddled heart.

Hush, Little Baby

It's no secret that I love babies. God has gifted us with eleven grandchildren, and fortunately, the inn has a playroom dedicated to dollies, cars, and trains.

This week I tackled the laundry heap created by seven dolls with their many outfit changes and blankets. I find a simple joy in caring for these toy babies and houses. You might guess where my thoughts are heading. May I humbly and courageously share these next few words that are near to my heart?

Our world around us has devalued human life. There is a war being waged in our country on the issue of abortion. Regardless of the political nature, I believe abortion is foremost a biblical and moral issue. God places value on human life. Babies, after all, are His design.

You made all the delicate, inner parts of my body
and knit me together in my mother's womb.
Thank you for making me so wonderfully complex!
Your workmanship is marvelous, how well I know it.

(Psalm 139:13–14 NLT)

We live in a heartbreaking world filled with stories of suffering. There is great controversy on both sides of the issue. It is overwhelming, and I don't pretend to have all the answers for all the hardships.

Here is what I do know: Jesus loves all babies, inside and outside the womb. They are precious in His sight, and He knows them by name.

As I write, God is displaying a magnificent sunrise, a reminder that beauty can be found in the midst of chaos and violence in our world. We only need to look.

Note: I understand this is a tender subject for some and an explosive subject for others. I'm always open to chatting and hearing your thoughts, and always, I'd be honored with your company.

You Are Cordially Invited

I'm working through an old brown hymnal as part of my morning breakfast with Jesus. What treasures I discover in this practice of singing through the hymns I was raised with.

Before I landed on the hymn of the day, my mind wandered to another breakfast with a most unusual invite. Jesus' friends, His disciples, were fishing on the Sea of Tiberias, not for recreation but for their livelihood. Jesus, who had just been resurrected, suddenly appeared to His friends.

And just as suddenly, friend John realized the man on the shore was Jesus. Peter, in his zeal, dove overboard to swim to shore. The other disciples arrived on shore to the aroma of breakfast.

After all the tumult leading up to the empty tomb and all the wonder of "What's next?" for the disciples, Jesus issued this beautiful four-word invitation: "Come and have breakfast" (John 21:12 NIV).

Jesus made a campfire. Jesus cooked. Jesus invited. Jesus ate with His friends.

My morning hymn from 1931, "Jesus, Revealed in Me," is unfamiliar, but these summarized words make a beautiful prayer. May I reflect His grace.

I am happiest when I take time to break bread with Jesus. It is a life-giving habit. Jesus helps clarify my agenda. He empowers my inadequacies. He provides direction. He gives me peace. My hands and feet move out as I get God's Word in.

I've set a lovely breakfast bouquet. There is room at the table for you. Come.

A Winning Mindset

It was overdue. Time to visit our internet and phone service contracts. Oh, the angst! Promotional deals that seem to be too good to be true. Halfway through one of the phone calls, I wondered, "Did that guy lie to me? What stops this guy from doing a side hustle with my credit card info in his basement?"

Hours into my research and calls and skepticism, I all but dove under the covers, giving up on the few dollars I envisioned us growing richer with. But alas, stubbornness helped push me through my negative mindset. Today we are happy owners of both new internet and phone services.

In all my hours on the phone, I ended one call with an apology. "I'm sorry for my frustration with you and your company policy." Under my breath, I really added "your ridiculous policy." But at the end of the day, that was a Jesus win. I held up my end of kindness in a quiet way amid great frustration. And I didn't give up.

Here is the win framed better by a big-hearted 1800s pastor:

I have all things and abound; not because I have a good store of money in the bank, not because I have skill and wit with which to win my bread, but because "The Lord is my Shepherd."

—Charles Spurgeon[7]

Jesus, he is my Shepherd, leading me of all places through the rough terrain of technology, of which I have neither skill nor wit.

It's a winning day here at the inn.

All in 7.5 Hours

Wonder. By definition it is a sense of awe and amazement, to marvel or ponder.

On a Thursday morning in a hectic week, I prepared my nook for a special time of wonder. It was a day off for me. I had a fresh cup of coffee, a lit cedar and balsam candle, my Bible and journal in hand, and a fire to keep me company. I was all set to wonder.

The phone rang.

Skip the coffee. Blow out the candle. Lace up my shoes. Innkeeper to caretaker. No time to wonder.

Hours later, I tiredly returned home from caring for my dear mom. The last thing on my agenda was a shower and changing into my pajamas. I had long forgotten wonder.

I curled up under my throw. The doorbell rang. Pajama-clad, I opened the door. No, it wasn't an Amazon delivery but a neighbor from around the bend, bearing banana bread and conversation. And there, under the dark sky, were a few unplanned moments with a new friend who needed a listening ear and to hear a whisper of Jesus' love.

My wondering needs cultivating. It is the ability to see God in the ordinary. This day, wonder arrived not in the way I expected but, rather, in a loaf of banana bread. In a mundane minute. In wet hair and pajamas.

It was God declaring that my Jesus-sharing matters. That night I found it mattered to a lady around the bend. So I keep telling the precious old story while Alexa plays strains of "Hark! The Herald Angels Sing."

A sense of wonder captured in a surprising way. It reminds me of another surprise visit long ago. Jesus, in a manger. A baby who came to rescue us. The event that changed history, and it changed my destiny.

I wonder.

Still Has Fallen

We are in that strange week after Christmas, when a lull has dropped in, waiting for a new year to open. With all the weeks of decorating, baking, shopping, traditionaling and gathering behind us ... the house is strangely quiet. And strangely enough, I find my heart is as well. After all the hustle and bustle of the month, I crave stillness.

There are no significant events on my planner. The refrigerator is emptied of holiday splurges, and the to-do list is far shorter. There is room for some short winter walks. And for fun, the new Bible study I will lead in January is on my worktable.

But I know before I can make the most of these last days on the calendar, I must first quiet my space. Undecorate. Pack three Christmas tubs. Dust. Vacuum. Mop. Redecorate.

And in a blink, the inn is redressed. With throws to snuggle under, we are ready for snow days. I still have some winter candles to burn.

Mrs. Tiggy-Winkle is a hedgehog washerwoman with kind and twinkly eyes. She launders the clothes of all the animals and generously delivers them clean and pressed.

—Beatrix Potter[8]

The year isn't over yet. End on a high note. It's not a new promise, but it is as fresh as the new day itself:

For he satisfies the longing soul.

(Psalm 107:9 ESV)

Only You, Jesus, can free our hearts and satisfy our longings.

Nighttime falls. Mrs. Tiggy-Winkle and I are ready for our cup of tea. Pressing clothes is hard work.

Housecleaning

I'll give you the definition and see if you can guess the word. Adjective—untidy or dirty; a confusing or difficult situation to deal with.

The word is *messy*. Although the inn could always use a bit more cleaning, the latter of that definition sits with me. I daresay we all have those situations that knock us for a loop, where a particular circumstance blindsides us. Right? I won't go into the details for privacy's sake, but what should we do when we are hit with a mess? How do we respond when a situation seemingly has little solution?

    A. Throw a pity party
    B. Breathe deeply and count to ten
    C. Stop at the store and buy mint ice cream
    D. Let feelings dictate the rest of the day

Far too often, C and D are my go-to's. Of course, neither provides a solution. In fact, both lead to more problems. It is one of the areas of life I have been working on. I have dubbed it "feelings management," which is as essential as weight management (hello, ice cream and M&M's). I'm working on both. It seems they are equally challenging.

I wait quietly before God,
for my victory comes from him.
He alone is my rock and my salvation,
my fortress where I will never be shaken.

(Psalm 62:1–2 NLT)

How does it work in this mess of mine? Rehearse these truths.

God is already ahead of this situation and working on it for good purposes. I can't see beyond the bend, but He does. He leans low and lovingly whispers, "Will you trust me with this?" And I say a wobbly yes.

This is on repeat until faith grows taller. And I find soul rest.

Trust makes the best walking stick if you've got something messy in your life that seems impossible. Lean in, take small steps, and get busy making your veggie tray.

'Tis Enough

When you are a Bear of Very Little Brain, and you Think of Things, you find sometimes that a Thing which seemed very Thingish inside you is quite different when it gets out into the open and has other people looking at it.

—A. A. Milne, *Winnie-the-Pooh*

If you are scratching your head wondering if this reading has a point, Innkeeper assures you it does. I sit with my notebook and calendar and ponder the past year while trying to figure out how to improve the view ahead.

I like to imagine the fresh, unwritten days ahead. In the rearview, I easily see God's blessings and find His faithfulness marked all over my failings. I think it is enough.

My social feed has all sorts of shoulds and tips to make the year ahead more meaningful and successful. Just today, in my email, there is a course about creating the life I always wanted offered for $99/month. Another email offers thirty-one days of daily core workouts.

I shrink a little. There are many wonderful ideas advertised while this innkeeper is just trying to lace up her tennis shoes.

And the view ahead? As much as I dream of waking up this new year, becoming grand and glorious with a whole new list of habit-keeping and adventure-seeking goals, I'm just banking on God's faithfulness. I think it is enough.

God's promises are good company. Hear these well-worn and beloved phrases:

> *The faithful love of the Lord never ends!*
> *His mercies never cease.*
> *Great is his faithfulness;*
> *his mercies begin afresh each morning.*

(Lamentations 3:22–23 NLT)

Mercies afresh for a fresh new year.

Hope is peeking around the corner. My tennies are on the move.

Beyond a Weather Report

As I was leaving Walmart in the snow, blow, and 26° below, or so it felt, I said these words out loud: "Love where you are." It was the middle of January in Ohio, and we had hit our first shovelable snow.

This quote was making its rounds on social media: "If you choose not to find joy in the snow, you will have less joy in your life but still the same amount of snow." Innkeeper smiles. Love where you are.

And it goes deeper than measurable snowfall. Contentment. The *1828 Webster's American Dictionary of the English Language* defines *contentment* as "a resting or satisfaction of mind without disquiet." Since *disquiet* is not a word oft spoken, I looked it up: uneasy, anxious, restless. I make my own dictionary entry. Contentment: a mind that rests and is at peace.

It's not easy to weather the storms of life, which often linger much longer than the most recent snowfall. I want a contentment that reaches beyond the weather. A mind at rest does more gratitude and less grumbling. More trusting, less fretting. More cookie baking, less criticizing.

A lofty goal? We can work on it together. This proverb is found in ancient words.

A heart at peace gives life to the body.

(Proverbs 14:30 NIV)

This heart is formed by the grace of God walking alongside the principles of truth.

A resting heart can walk through snowdrifts. It can also stroll on a white sandy beach.

PS: My love for snow days is a carryover from being married to a teacher. Our old answering machine's sweetest message in bygone days: "Mr. Deeks, school is canceled for tomorrow."

Light the candle and cue the music!

Two Words

For all the sad words of tongue and pen, the saddest are these: "It might have been." (Unknown author, "Don't Quit").

I paraphrase the unknown author: things go wrong, he trudges uphill, his funds are low, and his debts are high, all followed by a big ole sigh.

We can feel his pain in wanting to quit.

When I chose this sentiment for a custom-made bracelet, it seemed to bring good cheer into my season: don't quit your day.

It is tempting. Life gets tangled up. The day brings unwanted interruptions. We lose our focus. The weary heart says, "Skip the chores; it's time to veg out." The heart in need of cheer says, "Skip the chores; let's go shopping."

The author of Hebrews in the New Testament said, "Let us run with endurance the race that is set before us" (Hebrews 12:1 NASB).

There is the secret sauce to making the most of our days: actively pursue, get up, and move forward in what God has called you to. Just as God has hand-designed my race and yours, He gives us the strength to run it. Without discipline, we can dither our lives away.

One of my habits over the years is to keep appointments with God each morning. I read the Bible and talk over my day with Him. This single habit has been a guiding force for over fifty years.

It's a quiet repetition. First, you form the habit, and then your habit forms you. I have long sensed that there is growth in a routine.

Having said that, I am ready for a vacation where I can dither along for many days. Whatever your rhythms are or aren't, we Never Quitters walk together. And it makes my heart glad.

Tablescape

It's the wee hours of the morning and I'm listening to a song of surrender. How does it happen to my oft-wandering heart that I get so easily distracted? I chase after that which does not satisfy. I allow the words of fear to drown out the words of the Fear Conqueror.

Protecting heart-peace, one choice at a time, is my job. I open up the ancient words from the prophet Isaiah.

> *You will keep in perfect peace*
> *those whose minds are steadfast,*
> *because they trust in you.*

(Isaiah 26:3 NIV)

The definition of *steadfast*: an unswerving, unwavering, unfaltering trust in God. That is a lot of "uns." It is a tall order, especially in my unables and feelings of being unqualified.

What does a Bible study girl who feels unsettled do? Eat one more (extra-large) slice of chocolate chip bundt cake. In my experience, that helps for about thirty-three seconds and only adds to the unlovely.

Let's try to find a better answer. Fix my mind on Jesus and accept His invitation of perfect peace.

I pull up a chair to His banqueting table laden with courage, love, clarity, purpose, wisdom, security, forgiveness, and joy.

I choose to dine with Him today. Peace is served. I wouldn't be surprised to find a chocolate chip somewhere on that table!

Scissor Happy?

Salon trip day arrived. My hairdresser had relocated, so on a friend's recommendation, I chose a salon I was not familiar with. I was happy I had figured on spending extra money because as I walked in, I sensed I was in for a new experience. The salon had simple lines; immaculate, shining white floors; a beautiful wall waterfall (seriously!); and luxurious leather chairs.

I was offered dainty cookies, coffee, and a hand massage. Along with a polite no thank you to the refreshments, I learned lesson number one: don't prejudge on looks. Not entirely comfortable in such a fancy setting, I took my seat at station number four. To my dismay, my chair was smack dab in the middle of the most enormous floor-to-ceiling mirror I'd ever seen. My insecurities began to pile as high as the ceiling mirror.

I glanced around. I didn't notice any other customers filling their chairs quite so *roundly*. The more I looked around, the more out of place I felt. The hair snipping began, and with every clip, clip, clipping, my little brain said, "No fit, no fit, no fitting."

Convinced that this salon was a terrible idea, I quieted the voice in my head. Doing what I always do, I began asking hairdresser Amanda about her job. Then I steered the conversation to cooking and finally to her children. Eventually, the haircut was finished. Amanda had done an excellent job. And between all the snippings, I had made a new friend.

Lesson number two. We always fit, regardless of size, skin color, pocketbooks, or job titles . . . "The rich and the poor have a common bond; the Lord is the Maker of them all" (Proverbs 22:2 AMP).

We are made in God's image. We are all unique and precious, every one of us.

I never returned to that salon, but it stands in my memory as a special place. My credit card paid for not just a haircut but two lovely lessons. It was a perfect fit.

What Can $2 Buy You?

As it turns out, a finished bedroom.

On a random Friday, my Bible study friends and I walked to an estate sale in our neighborhood. I'm not a regular shopper of estates, but this was a nice walk. Amongst all the clutter (and, in my perception, a lot of junk), I spotted a distressed shelf.

From the crowded basement, the humble little shelf whispered she needed a new home. And I listened. "Two dollars," said the blue tape and cash lady. I returned to Wander Inn to a blank wall, a wall still empty, waiting for that specific something.

After a thorough cleaning, I presented Humble Shelf to my husband, who is well familiar with my brainstorms. Minutes later, the shelf was up, complete with added decor. Our bare wall was exceedingly happy. The shelf sighed in contentment.

> *The power of finding beauty in the humblest things makes home happy and life lovely.*
>
> —Louisa May Alcott[9]

Oh, Louisa, you are my kindred spirit. Sometimes, when you least expect it, inspiration comes. It might just be hidden under a lot of clutter and a whole lot of dirt.

A noble yearning. Cultivate a meaningful life that prefers simplicity and kindness, smallness and integrity. Pursue Jesus and delight in His friendship.

Do you have a tiny spark? A small movement that can push you through a different door? Small can be significant. At Wander Inn, I'm fluffing and folding, tending to a rhythm of habit that fortifies.

I read Psalm 25 this morning: "Show me the right path, O Lord, point out the road for me to follow, lead me by your truth and teach me" (Psalm 25:4–5 NLT). These words are my prayer. A prayer that keeps and holds my heart.

Once upon a time . . . a tiny $2 choice reflected the grand ambition to finish off a bedroom. I'm living big in our small inn.

Inn Play

When I was young, some of my favorite tales I enjoyed came from Grimm's Fairy Tales. I remember a story about a maiden living in a cottage who kept herself busy spinning and weaving and bringing cow parsley from the meadow.

What do you do to inject some sunshine into your day? Assuming you're not gathering cow parsley, I'll guess it has something to do with creating—making music, gardening, baking, painting, building, crafting, etc.

In need of a "flip the script" in my mind, I created. I had one criterion in mind. It needed to be something easy, quick, and inexpensive. My creation only required three items: white beans, a vase, and a candle. Ready. Fill the small vase with white beans, nestle the white candle into the beans, light the candle, and yes! The total cost was $1.48 and twenty-two minutes. My counter was graced with a lovely sweetness.

Create: "to form anew; to change the state or character, to renew" (*1828 Webster's American Dictionary of the English Language*).

Ever wonder why we enjoy creating so much? Why working with our hands brings us joy? I'm pretty sure it is a proven fact that when your hands are full of energy and creativity, your heart beats happier.

In the beginning God created.

(Genesis 1:1 NIV)

God is the Master Creator and Designer. On the days you don't feel like much of a something, remember this:

We are his workmanship,
created in Christ Jesus for good works.

(Ephesians 2:10 ESV)

This is a simple, beautiful truth: you and I are God's masterpieces. So, my friend, walk a little taller today while gathering your cow parsley.

Spin a Story

After our downsizing move, I decided to take up biking again. (Backstory—I love riding bikes, but after breaks to my ankle and foot bones, I was no longer confident of my balance on a two-wheeler.) Our house move had placed us where we could walk and bike down the middle of our street.

My husband bought me a purple three-wheeler with a white basket for my birthday. I named it Grapesicle.

We immediately became friends. Grapesicle and I took off, flying through all our little streets and waving at people in our neighborhood. It was love at first sight. Oh, the many happy summer hours of riding.

And then I woke up from my delightful dream.

The tale hit a first bump in the road when my physically fit husband took the three-wheeler for its first spin. After a trial run, these were his exact words: "It's going to take some getting used to." His words might have been an understatement of my year. Looking back, I missed a clue.

But ever the optimist, I thought, *How hard could this be?*

I jumped on Grapesicle and headed for my first spin. I could not have been more wrong. I barely made it around one loop, huffing and puffing. Deflated, I had to admit (1) I wasn't in any physical shape to handle this heavy bike and (2) this bike did not offer the security from falling I was looking for. Grapesicle and I sadly parted company.

But not to be deterred, I had another dream—this time on my old $89 Walmart bike, which I have not named. I'm working on getting back in shape with high hopes of this dream coming true.

Come summertime, if you're in my area, you may spot me flying through the streets. Wave. I'll wave back.

Oats, Beans, and Barley

Thanks to the internet, I found the tune playing in my head. I remember, as a child, an old song about oats. After some fun research, I found it. Maybe it will be familiar to you?

It is a folk song that traveled from Britain to America. It is an action song that tells a story and is meant for children to perform.

Oats and beans and barley grow.
Oats and beans and barley grow.
Can you or I or anyone know how oats and beans and barley grow?

The rest of the song continues with several verses. The farmer is the hero. He sows the seeds. He waters the seeds. He hoes the weeds, and finally, he harvests the seeds.

Whew! That farmer worked hard just so I could open the round Quaker box and enjoy my steel-cut oats with seven frozen blueberries. It's a breakfast of champions. Thank you, Farmer Ben.

Just as the farmer found it to be true, there are rhythms to our lives that run on routines. And routines are good for the soul. They require rigorous discipline from within.

As already stated, I have found the habit of engaging with God each morning to be valuable in my life. It is a grounding habit that I began as a teenager. My goal is not to get up at an appointed time to read a particular number of verses or to pray for a certain amount of time. The goal is a lifelong habit of walking with God daily. What peace and joy it gives me to bring my family, my dreams, my fears, and my worries before Jesus. What direction God provides for the day ahead as I open His letter.

I invite you to join my morning routine: oats and the Bible.

Good Enough?

Seeing a friend make cute mini cake pops, I made an impulsive Amazon purchase. This little purple cake pop machine arrived in time to help celebrate our grandson's birthday. I went to work on phase one.

It was easy, considering I was an amateur at cake pops. (One disappointing find—you can't use a box cake; you need to make a cake from scratch, using their recipes.) So red velvet cake it was. When all the cake balls were baked and cooled, I popped them into the freezer, awaiting phase two.

I assembled my workstation the morning of the party, enlisting my husband's help. (In my experience, having a level-headed brain working in tandem with my brain is an advantage.)

Step 1: Microwave the marshmallow store-bought icing in a coffee mug. Step 2: Insert a lollipop stick into the cake balls, dip into the icing, then dust with sprinkles. Step 3: This is where the cake balls and I fell apart. My second impulsive buy with the purple machine was a pink cake pop holder, which, in my defense, looked perfect in the picture.

I will spare you the angst of my $11 purchase, but it was a waste of money. I later returned to my Amazon order, and had I read the description, I'd have saved $11 and avoided the phase two disaster, which might be a strong word, except it wasn't. Even Mr. Level-head was running out of patience. Dilemma: how to prop up these decorated cake pops? After several failed attempts, we were left with plating them, meaning they ended up being flat-bottomed cake pops.

At party time, I artfully arranged them. Cue the birthday tune. The cake pops were a big hit! No one said anything about the flat pops.

Is there a moral to my story? Yes, there is no pressure to make perfect cake pops. After all, I was making these for children ages seven and under. My stress to form perfect cake pops was in overdrive.

I'm grateful perfection is not needed in the biggest arena of my life. One day, when my life is over, I have a reservation waiting in heaven with my name on it. It's a move up, and it is not based on my performance. Heaven is real; many of my family and friends are already there. My best friend and Savior, Jesus, stands with His arms open wide, accepting reservations.

Won't I be surprised if cake pops are on the menu?

A Timely Perspective

Last summer I bought a timer on Amazon for $19.95 for my grandchildren. It worked wonders for tracking their playtime. Little did I know it would also benefit me. The un-techy timer, unattached to my phone and Alexa alarms, is heavenly.

I have a writing and studying corner in our nook. It reminds me a bit of Cinderella, who sang in her own little corner and chair.

With the fire going and coffee in hand, I can get lost in time. I set the timer for sixty minutes. Four ding dings and it's time to walk a few laps. Thank you, blue timer.

I crafted a verse onto the wooden lid of a broken enamel box. I tried my hand at tea staining the edges of the card. It looks sweet. The verse is sweeter.

If you, like me, are tackling something bigger than you can muster, take comfort in God's promise:

For God is working in you, giving you the desire
and the power to do what pleases him.

(Philippians 2:13 NLT)

Cinderella, the classic fairy tale, is a timeless story of virtue rewarded. She wins the charming prince and lives happily ever after.

While I have already won my prince, I hope the little blue timer is a rewarder of my goals, the big and little ones.

No pressure, little timer.

A Bloom Speaks

When we bought our house in disrepair, a bush in our backyard was in bloom. I used LeafSnap, an app I installed on my phone, to identify the plant. It is a Japanese Snowball bush. Snowball lent me hope that beauty could be restored.

This beautiful bush carries dainty white cascading flowers that bloom from spring through fall. It is in my direct line of vision from my nook and provides the perfect resting spot for birds visiting our feeders.

In my mind, this bush connects me to the first owner of our home. I wonder about the lady who planted it. (I guess it could have been a man, but my dream works better with a lady.) Is she still living? I was told she had a baby grand piano in the living room.

When she planted that small bush in the soil many years ago, she had no idea that an innkeeper would someday come along to redeem her home and restore it to its former beauty.

I would love to sit with the original owner and share our ambitions, loves, and worries. After a hundred questions were answered and our teacups were drained, I would say thank you with a hug. I would thank her for sowing beauty for me to enjoy, beauty in the form of a Japanese

Snowball. And I would ask her if she was acquainted with my friend Jesus.

The visit would be too short.

My dream ends with this question: What am I sowing of beauty?

Adoniram Judson, an American missionary to Burma, said, "A life once spent is irrevocable."[10]

What am I planting that will outlive me? What am I building that makes a difference now and will matter in eternity?

Like the delicate flowers of my Snowball bush are pleasantly fragrant, so I pray my life is.

Fellow Pilgrims

We are traveling forward, though this book is coming to an end. You and I aren't staying where we are today. Thomas Aquinas described Christians as *homo viator,*[11] pilgrims on the journey, humans on the way.

On my journey I have no illusions about having arrived. Learning to be like Jesus is a lifelong pursuit.

I heard an old-time gospel preacher share something like this: care more for a grain of faith than a ton of excitement. From the first, my passion for writing this book has been about merging together faith and excitement. I hope you caught it in my words: life becomes extraordinary lived with Jesus.

Our backpacks are loaded with all we need: our Bible as our map and Jesus as our traveling companion for the path ahead.

I tucked a little something extra into your backpack. Through these pages, I've not kept my struggles with fear and feelings of inadequacy a secret. These four God declarations are well-worn and tattered from use.

1. "You are mine" (Isaiah 43:1 NIV).
2. "You are free" (1 Peter 2:16 NLT).
3. "[You] are more than conquerors" (Romans 8:37 ESV).
4. "Don't be afraid, I am here!" (John 6:20 NLT).

Lace up your tennies, friend. There are more trails ahead.

If you would like to continue on this journey with me, you can follow and add your own thoughts at smallthoughts.blog.

Afterword

The title of this section is a common way to end a book. It also fits as the last and most important thoughts I share with you: you can be sure of heaven.

1. God's purpose for us is life and peace. That is the good news of the Bible. The God of the universe created us to be loved by Him and to know Him personally, now and for all eternity.
2. The bad news is that we are broken and sinful. When we choose by active rebellion or passive indifference to reject God, we are separated from Him. We cannot fix ourselves. "For all have sinned and fall short of the glory of God" (Romans 3:23 NIV).
3. The Bible makes it clear we cannot save ourselves: not by attending church, not by doing good deeds, and not even by reading the Bible. We cannot earn our way into heaven. Because God is holy, He cannot allow sin to enter heaven. How, then, can we be saved from our sin? "For it is by grace you have been saved, through faith—and this is not from yourselves, it is the gift of God—not by works so that no one can boast" (Ephesians 2:8–9 NIV).

4. Back to the good news. In spite of our sins, Jesus died for us. "But God demonstrates his own love for us in this: While we were still sinners, Christ died for us" (Romans 5:8 NIV).

5. Jesus died on the cross for our sins to free us from the guilt and judgment of sin. He rose from the grave, breaking the power of death and making a way for us to have eternal life in heaven.

6. Responding to God's gift by faith is as simple as praying the following prayer:

"Jesus, I believe that you love me and that you died and rose so I could be forgiven and come to know you. I confess I have sinned against you and ask you to forgive me. I ask you to come into my heart and be the Lord of my life. I trust you with everything, and I thank you for loving me so much that I can know you here on earth and spend the rest of eternity with you in heaven."

PS: There are many choice points along life's way. This is one of them. It is a choice so sacred that it affects all eternity. Should you choose Jesus as your Savior, let the celebration begin! You are saved.

Knowing God's peace, perspective, and purpose for your life begins with a personal relationship with Jesus. This is just the beginning! There are many resources to help you grow in your new life in Christ.

If you choose to ask Jesus to save you, I'm shouting a hallelujah! I would love to hear from you. If you are interested in the next steps you can take or have any questions, please feel free to contact me. I count it a privilege. (My contact information is on the back of this book.)

Endnotes

1. Mark Noll, "Resolutions of Jonathan Edwards," Christian History Institute, accessed April 26, 2024, https://christianhistoryinstitute.org/magazine/article/resolutions-of-jonathan-edwards.

2. A. A. Milne, *Winnie the Pooh* (New York, New York: Sky Pony, 2023).

3. Louisa May Alcott, "My Kingdom," Discovery Poetry, accessed April 26, 2024, https://discoverpoetry.com/poems/louisa-may-alcott/my-kingdom/.

4. William Shakespeare, *Hamlet*, act 1, scene 3, line 564.

5. George Müller, Soul Nourishment First, George Müller website, accessed April 26, 2024, https://www.georgemuller.org/soul-nourishment-first.html.

6. Arthur Pierson, *The Crisis of Missions: Or the Voice out of the Cloud* (New York: Robert Carter and Brothers, 1886).

7. Ethan Collins, "The Pearl of the Psalms: Spurgeon on Psalm 23," The Spurgeon Center, November 27, 2020, https://www.spurgeon.org/resource-library/blog-entries/the-pearl-of-the-psalms-spurgeon-on-psalm-23/.

8. Beatrix Potter, *The Tale of Mrs. Tiggy-Winkle* (London: Frederick Warne & Company, 1905).

9. Louisa May Alcott, *Little Women* (Boston: Roberts Brothers, 1868).

10. Adoniram Judson, *The Life of Adoniram Judson* (New York: Anson, Randolph & Company, 1883).

11. Thomas Aquinas, *Summa Theologica Part I-II* (Cincinnati, OH: Benzinger Brothers, 2010).